Orange Judd

The Kitchen

Or Every-Day Cookery, Containing Many Useful, Practical Directions,

Recipes, etc.

Orange Judd

The Kitchen

Or Every-Day Cookery, Containing Many Useful, Practical Directions, Recipes, etc.

ISBN/EAN: 9783744789981

Printed in Europe, USA, Canada, Australia, Japan

Cover: Foto ©Lupo / pixelio.de

More available books at **www.hansebooks.com**

THE KITCHEN;

OR,

EVERY-DAY COOKERY,

CONTAINING MANY USEFUL

PRACTICAL DIRECTIONS, RECIPES, ETC.

WITH NUMEROUS WOOD ENGRAVINGS

SHOWING HOW TO CARVE,

AND THE

PROPER MODE OF SENDING DISHES TO TABLE.

A Companion Volume to Rand, McNally & Co.'s Pocket Cyclopedia.

CHICAGO:
RAND, McNALLY & COMPANY.
1885.

PREFACE.

A great want will be met by this carefully prepared, condensed yet very comprehensive volume. It embraces, in small compass, directions for every Department of Preparing and Cooking Food, from the cutting block to the dessert, including Carving and Serving. It is intended to meet the necessities of all classes of housekeepers—those living on plain, simple food, and those requiring more costly dishes.

A marked feature, however, is, that instead of giving a great number of recipes, etc., with quantities stated in brief form as only, a smaller number of choice ones are selected, and the best and method of combining the materials, upon which the good quality often largely depends, are stated so plainly as to meet the wants of the most inexperienced housekeepers.

Every house provider should know how to select and order the different cuts of meats from the butcher. We therefore give illustrations of the mode of cutting up the carcass, and the names and the use made of the different pieces.

Carving, in the best manner, is an art that comparatively few possess, and to aid the novice in this, we present sundry illustrative engravings and directions. A simple dish, judiciously prepared and properly carved and served, is more tasteful, more appetizing and more acceptable, than a much more costly one displayed without taste, and served in a bungling manner. We present some Garnished Dishes, suggestive of what can be done to make the table attractive.

In the preparation of the volume the Author has consulted various American and Foreign Works on Cooking and Housekeeping, and some professional Cooks of high standing, and gathered from these various sources the best materials, according to her judgment, aided by long practical experience and observation at home and abroad.

The Publishers confidently believe this Hand Book will prove both acceptable, and exceedingly valuable in every AMERICAN HOME.

CONTENTS.

	PAGE
ABOUT CARVING,	5–21
BEEF,	32–35
BREAKFAST ROLLS, ETC.,	64–67
CAKES,	82–88
CATSUPS,	57
DISHES FOR DESSERT,	75–77
EGGS,	95
FISH,	27–31
GAME,	48–53
JAMS AND JELLIES,	89, 90
MISCELLANEOUS,	101–104
MUTTON,	40–42
OYSTERS,	54–56
PICKLES,	92–94
PIES, TARTS, ETC.,	78–81
PORK,	39
POULTRY,	43–47
PRESERVING FRUIT,	91
PUDDINGS,	68–73
SALADS,	58–60
SAUCES,	74
SOUPS,	22–26
VEAL,	36–38
VEGETABLES,	96–100
YEAST AND BREAD,	61–63

ABOUT CARVING.

Directions.

At a public dinner an eminent man of letters was attempting to carve a turkey of somewhat uncertain age, when his fork slipped and the bird slid into the lap of a distinguished lady sitting opposite. Without seeming to be at all disturbed or disconcerted, he held out the platter in both hands and said, quite courteously, "Madam, I'll thank you for that turkey." Not many men are endowed with this degree of coolness under such circumstances. There are few persons who are so thoroughly skilled in table dissection as not to be embarrassed on being called upon to carve when surrounded by a company of strangers, or even friends.

We present a few directions for some of the more difficult operations. In our observations abroad, and in looking through a considerable number of English and French books on cooking and carving, to gather the best materials from all sources for this Manual, we have found that foreign customs are somewhat different from those prevalent in this country. For example, the larger English books, whose writers are less accustomed to our great American table-fowl—the turkey—direct to stuff only the breast; to lay the legs and wings close to the body, tying the former partly into the posterior cavity. Then in carving, it is directed to cut for the guests only from the breast, and to leave the entire legs and wings for the servants. In this country it is customary in cooking to stuff the entire cavity of the body, to lay the wings close to it, and to simply tie the ends of the limbs above. The bird is brought to the table thus, lying squarely upon its back. Then, in serving, the "second joint" of the leg, that part nearest the body, is esteemed the choicest part, and to be offered to those entitled to most consideration, unless a preference is expressed for white meat only. If no preference is given, it is usual to serve a portion of both the breast and the second joint. A part of the wing is preferred by some. In fact, the most delicate parts are in two little muscles lying in small dish-like cavities on each side of the back, a little behind the leg attachments. The next most delicate meat fills the cavities in the neck-bone, and next to this, that on the second joints. The white breast meat is comparatively dry and flavorless.

Beef.

The manner of cutting up a side of beef is shown in the engraving on page 7. The muscles on the parts of the animal least used are the most tender and juicy, and are found along the back from the rump to the back part of the shoulder, while the shoulder, neck and limbs are the toughest and least desirable. The names of the several joints in the hind and fore quarters, and their uses, are as follows:

Hind Quarter: 1. Sirloin; this includes the tenderloin on the part toward 9, separated from the sirloin proper by a few steaks termed pin steaks. 2. Rump; a prime part for steaks. 3. Aitchbone; a good boiling piece. 4. Buttock; prime boiling piece. 5. Mouse-round; boiling or stewing. 6. Hock; soup piece or stewing. 7. Thick flank, cut with the udder fat; primest boiling piece. 8. Thin flank; boiling.

Fore Quarter: 9. Five ribs, called the fore-rib; this is considered the best roasting piece. 10. Four ribs, called the middle-rib; greatly esteemed by housekeepers as the most economical piece for roasting. 11. Two ribs, called the chuck-rib; used for second quality of steaks. 12. Leg-of-mutton piece ; the muscles of the shoulder dissected from the breast. 13. Brisket, or breast ; used for boiling after being salted. 14. Neck, clod and sticking-piece ; used for soups, gravies, stocks, pies, sausages, etc. 15. Shin ; soups, stewing.

The different pieces vary greatly in price, where there is a large call for "choice cuts."

The following is a classification of the qualities of the several joints, as cut up, by this illustration :

First Class. — Includes the sirloin, the tenderloin, with the kidney suet (1), the rump-steak piece (2), the fore-rib (9).

Second Class. — The buttock (4), the thick flank (7), the middle-rib (10).

Third Class. — The aitchbone (3), the mouse-round (5), the thin flank (8), the chuck (11), the leg-of-mutton piece (12), the brisket (13).

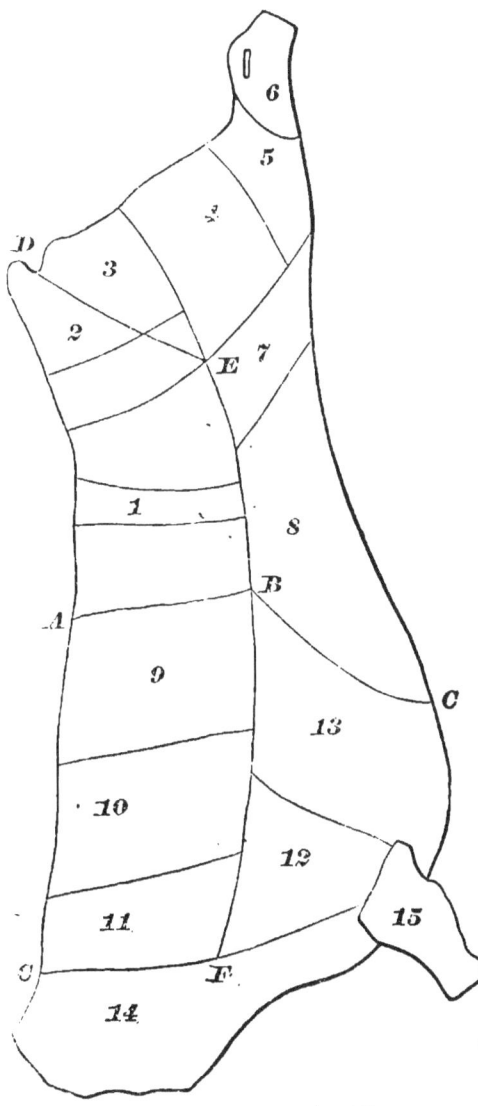

Fig. 1. Showing a Side of Beef.

Fourth Class.—The neck, clod and sticking-piece (14).
Fifth Class.—The hock (6), the shin (15).

Veal.

The carcass is divided into four quarters, with twelve ribs to each fore quarter, and these quarters are again subdivided into joints, as shown in the figure.

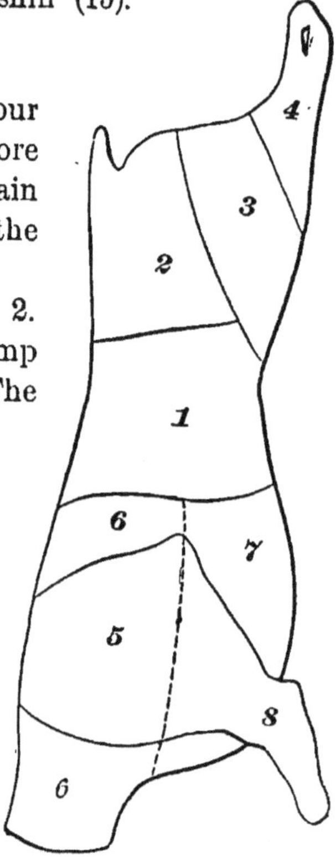

Hind Quarter: 1. The loin. 2. The chump, consisting of the rump and hock-bone. 3. The fillet. 4. The hock, or hind-knuckle.

Fore Quarter: 5. The shoulder. 6,6. The neck. 7. The breast. 8. The fore-knuckle.

The several parts of a well-fed calf, not over fat, are nearly of the following weights: loin and chump, 18 pounds; fillet, 12½ pounds; hind-knuckle 5½ pounds; shoulder, 11 pounds; neck, 11 pounds; breast, 9 pounds; fore-knuckle, 5 pounds; making a total of 144 pounds weight.

Fig. 2. Side of a Calf, showing the several joints.

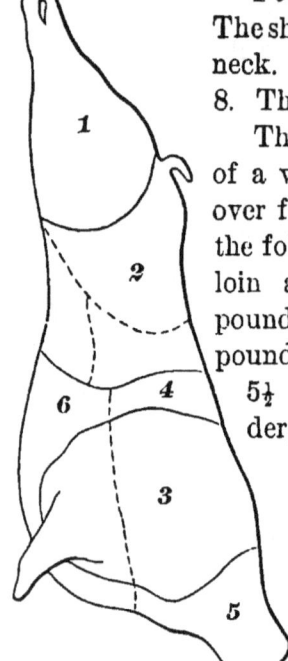

Fig. 3. A Side of Mutton, showing the joints.

Mutton.

Separate the hind from the fore quarters, leaving eleven ribs to the latter. The quarters are again subdivided as follows:

Cutting up Meats.

Hind Quarter: 1. The leg. 2. The loin. The two loins when in one piece are called the saddle. *Fore Quarter:* 3. The shoulder. 4 and 5. The neck. 5 is also called the scrag, which is commonly separated from 4, the lower and better joint. 6. The breast. The haunch of mutton comprises all the leg and as much of the loin short of the rib or lap as is indicated on the upper part, or 2, by a dotted line.

Pork.

First, as to cutting up the carcass. The general practice is first to cut off the head and then split the carcass lengthwise through the spinal column. The hams and shoulders marked in the illustrations 1 and 4 are usually cured. The sides are divided into hind and fore quarters.

The parts of the hind quarter are: 1. The leg. 2. The loin. 3. The spring (or belly). Parts of the fore quarter are: 4. The hand or shoulder. 5. The fore loin. 6. The cheek.

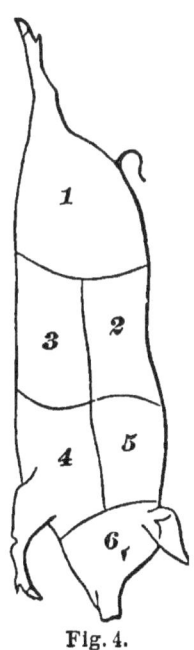

Fig. 4.

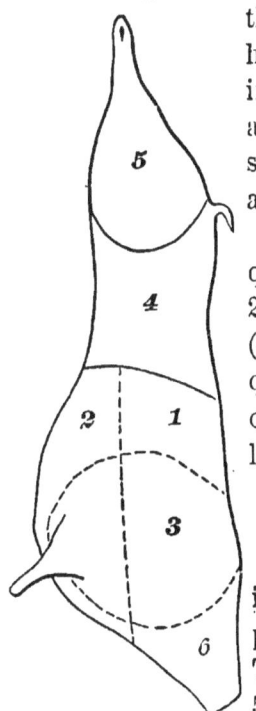

Fig. 5. Showing a Side of Lamb.

Lamb.

The mode of cutting up a side of lamb is almost the same as in mutton. The parts are thus designated: 1. The ribs. 2. The breast. 3. The shoulder. 4. The loin. 5. The leg. 6. The neck.

Nos. 1, 2, 3 belong to the fore quarter.

The Kitchen.

In order to obtain the flavor of lamb in perfection, it shou'd not be long kept. In purchasing for the table there are certain signs by which one can judge very accurately whether it has been long kept or not. If recently killed, the eye should be bright and dilated, and the quality of the fore quarter can be determined by the blue or healthy ruddiness of the jugular, or vein of the neck; while the firm, compact feel of the kidney will answer in an equally positive manner for the goodness of the hind quarter.

Beef Sirloin.

The usual mode of serving this choice piece is as here represented, though some prefer the fillet—called also, undercut and tenderloin—laid uppermost. The upper part should be cut in thin, even slices in the direction of the lines 5 to 6, and care should be taken to serve each guest to some of the

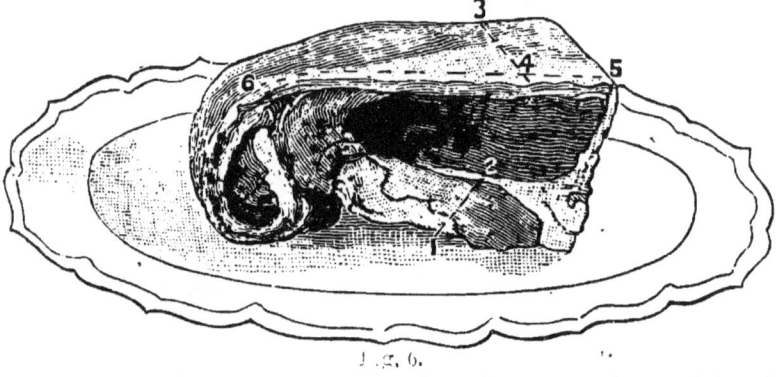

fat with the lean unless it is found to be distasteful. A wasteful method, adopted by some, is to carve this piece in the direction of 3 to 4. The fillet, very much preferred by many, is much best eaten hot, hence should be served at once. The slices may be cut in the direction of 1 to 2. To do this easily, the piece should first be raised. It will be found a great assistance in carving this joint well, to insert the knife just above the bone at the bottom and run sharply along, dividing the meat from the bone at the bottom and side.

Rib Roast.

This piece resembles the sirloin, except that it has no tenderloin, and the mode of carving is the same, *i.e.*, in the direction of the lines 1 to 2. This piece will be more easily cut if

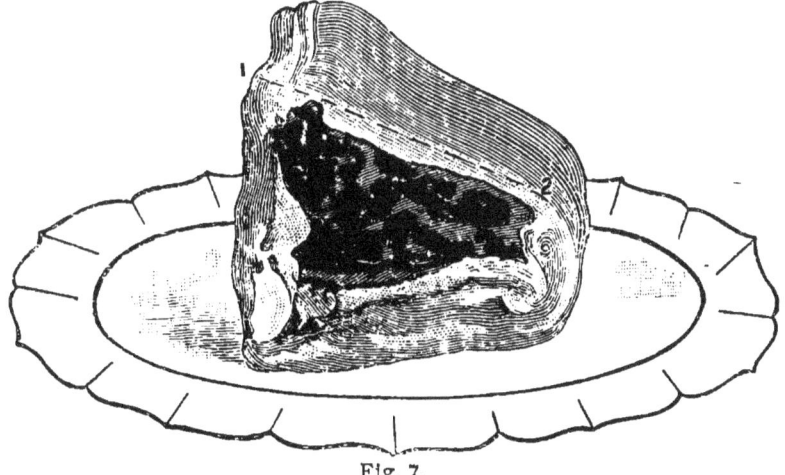

Fig. 7.

the plan be pursued which is suggested in carving the sirloin. Insert the knife between the bone and the meat, and separate them before beginning to cut it into slices. Let these always be thin and as even as possible.

Saddle of Mutton.

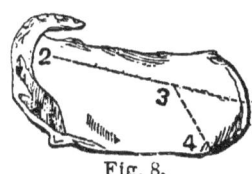

Fig. 8.

The carving of this joint is not difficult: it is usually cut in the direction of the line from 2 to 1, quite down to the bones in evenly cut slices. Some, however, carve it obliquely in the direction of 4 to 3, in which case the joint should be turned round, bringing the tail end to the right of the carver.

Haunch of Mutton.

A deep cut should first be made quite down to the bone, across the knuckle end of the joint, along the line 1 to 2. This will let the gravy escape, and then it may be carved in

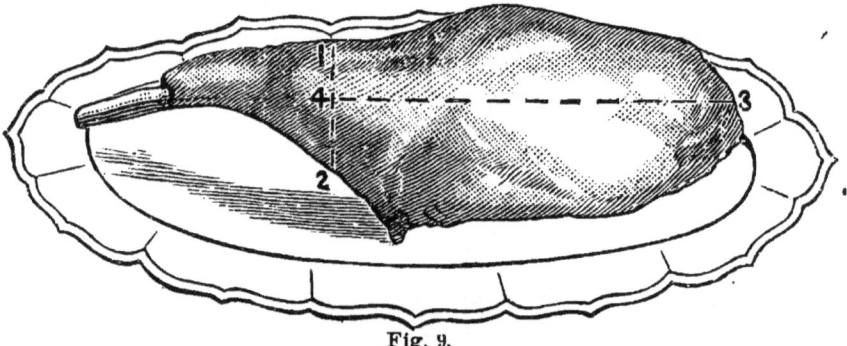

Fig. 9.

not too thick slices along the whole length of the haunch in the direction of the line from 4 to 3.

A haunch of venison is carved in a similar manner.

Leg of Mutton.

Wether mutton is most esteemed, and may be known by a lump of fat at the edge of the broadest part of the leg. The finest slices are to be obtained from the centre by carrying the knife sharply down in the direction of 1 to 2, and slices

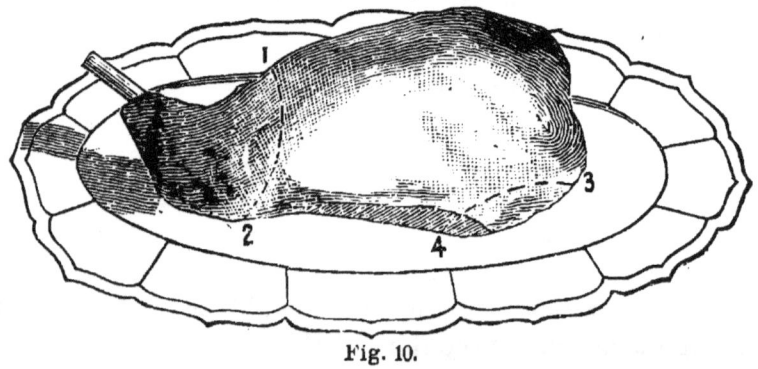

Fig. 10.

About Carving.

may be taken from either side, as the guests may desire, some preferring it underdone, others the reverse. The fat may be found near the lines 3 to 4. Some prefer to have this joint brought to the table with the underside uppermost, so as to get at the finely grained meat lying under that part of the joint known as the Pope's eye. Some also prefer the knuckle, and others the cramp bone, which is found by cutting down to the top of the thigh bone and running the knife under it in a semicircular direction toward the joint. When sent to the table a frill of paper around the knuckle will improve its appearance.

A leg of lamb, though much smaller than the mutton, may be carved in the same manner.

Fore Quarter of Lamb.

There is a little field for the carver's skill in separating the shoulder from the breast in the manipulation of this joint. Pass the knife in the direction of the dotted lines 1, 2, 3, 4, and

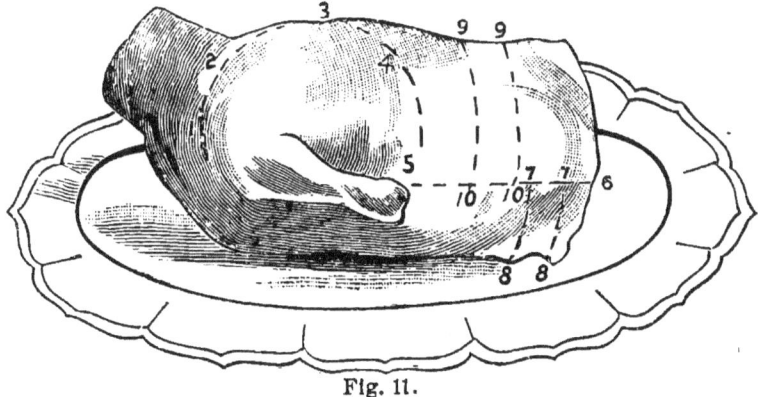

Fig. 11.

5, so as to cut through the skin, and then, with a little force, raising the shoulder, into which the fork should be firmly fixed, it will come away with a little more exercise of the knife. Care should be taken in removing the shoulder not to take too much meat from the breast and thus spoil its appearance. Next separate the ribs from the brisket, by cutting in the line 5 to 6. The ribs may be carved in the direction of the lines 9 to 10, and the brisket from 7 to 8. The carver should always ask the guests whether they prefer ribs, brisket, or a piece of the shoulder.

Calf's Head.

This is not the most easy dish to carve when first attempted, but a few directions will make it plain. Insert the knife down to the bone, and cut slices in the direction of 1 to 2. Serve with each of these a slice of the throat sweet-bread, cut in the

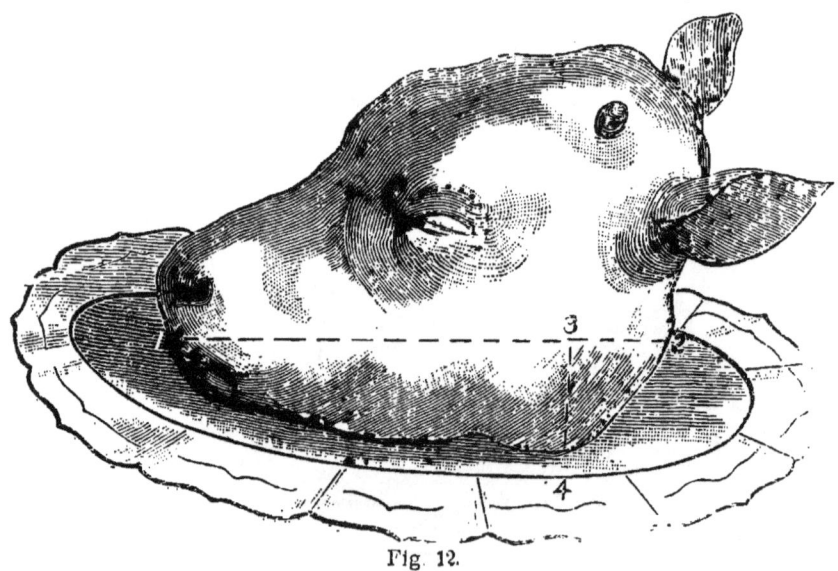

Fig. 12.

direction of 3 to 4. The eye and the flesh round it are considered dainty morsels with many, and should be given to those of the guests who are the greatest connoisseurs. To get at the eye, thrust the knife down on one side to the bottom of the socket and cut it quite round. The palate, or roof of the mouth, is also considered a great delicacy, and some fine lean will be found on the lower jaw, and nice gristly fat about the ear. The tongue and brains should be served in a separate dish, and each guest should be asked to take some of them.

Knuckle of Veal.

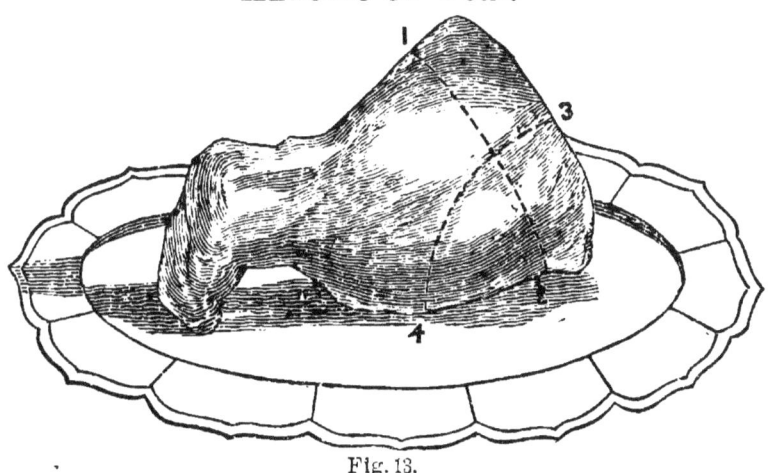

Fig. 13.

The dotted line, 1 to 2 in the above, shows the direction which should be given to the knife in carving this dish. The most choice cuts lie on the outside of the dotted line. The most delicate fat lies about the part 4, and if cut in a line from 3 to 4, the two bones, between which the fat lies, will be divided.

Ham.

To reach the choicer portion of a ham, the knife, which must be very sharp and thin, should be carried quite down to the bone in the direction of 1 to 2. The slices should be thin and even, and have some of the fat with the lean. Some cut a circular hole in the middle of the ham, gradually enlarging it outwardly; and others, who consult economy, begin at the hock-end and proceed onward till all is cut up. It

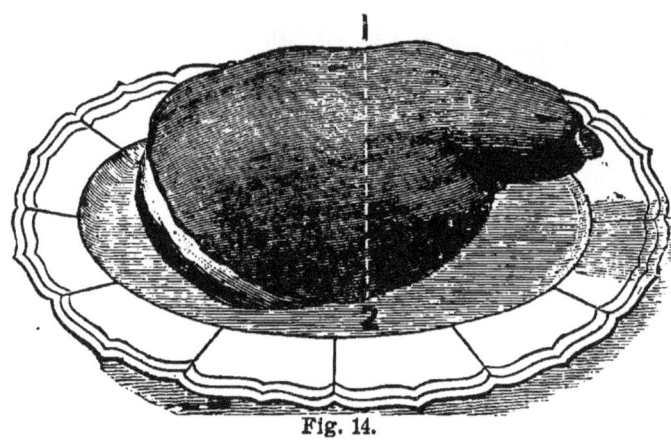

Fig. 14.

should be sent to the table with a paper frill around the knuckle.

A leg of roast pork is carved in the same manner as the ham.

Roast Pig.

A sucking pig is usually sent to the table as shown herewith, with the head detached, and both this and the body parted down the middle. Place the sides of the pig back to back in the dish, with one-half of the head and one of the ears at each end, and send to the table as hot as possible. Separate the shoulder from the carcass by carrying the knife around in the direction of the lines 1, 2, 3. The leg is next removed in the same manner as the shoulder, by cutting around the joint at 1, 2, 3. Separate the ribs into convenient

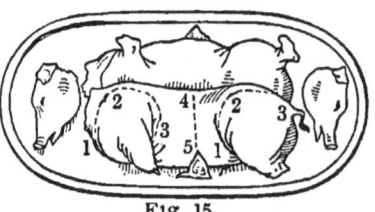

Fig. 15.

portions, in the direction of the line 4 to 5. The brains can now be taken out and served with the gravy and stuffing. Let the guests choose such parts as they prefer. The triangular part of the neck is by many considered the most delicate, but some prefer the ribs, and others the shoulders. The larger

About Carving.

parts are usually reserved for the gentlemen. The tongue and brains are often served on a separate dish.

Roast Turkey.

Bring the turkey to the table, as represented below, with the head to the right hand of the carver. Fix the fork firmly in the breast, just forward of 2. First sever the legs and wings on both sides, if the whole is to be carved, cutting neatly through the joint next the body. Then cut slices from the breast in the direction of the lines 2, 3, beginning on the lower part, and laying the pieces neatly on the side of the platter. Then unjoint the legs and wings at the middle joint,

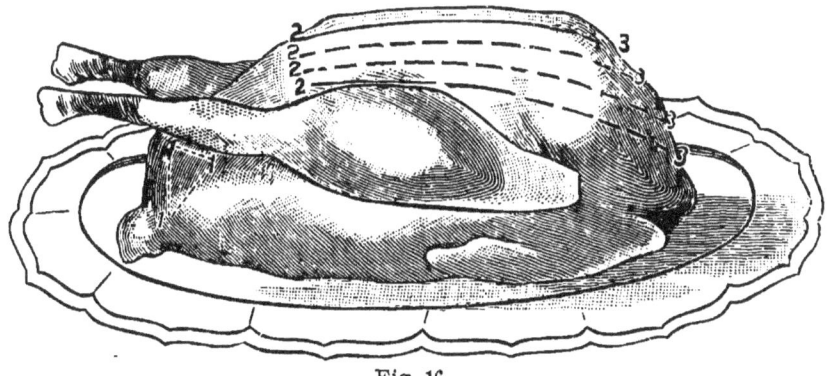

Fig. 16.

which can be struck almost exactly by an expert carver, or after a little practice. Consult the tastes of the guests as to which part is preferred. If no preference is expressed, serve a portion of both light and dark meat. Cut a piece from the rear part (1, 1), called the apron, and expose the dressing, to which each should be served, unless it is declined in advance.

NOTE.—The dressing is more readily accessible if the bird is placed with the head to the left. (See page 6.)

The Kitchen.

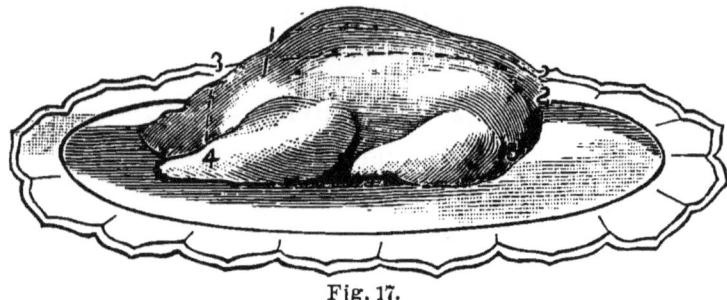

Fig. 17.

Roast Goose.

A little more dexterity and force are needed to carve a goose than some other fowls ; the beginning of the task, however, is not a difficult one. Carve evenly-cut slices from the breast in the direction of 2 to 3. Remove the apron by cutting in the line 1, 1, to get at the stuffing, here located, some of which should be served to each guest unless it is not desired. The carver should make as many breast slices as possible, and then remove the wings and legs. This may be done by turning the goose on one side and putting the fork through the small end of the leg bone and pressing it close to the body, which, when the knife enters at the upper side, raises the joint ; the knife is then to be passed under the joint, loosening the thigh bone from the socket. To remove the wing, put the fork into the small end of the pinion, and, pressing it closely to the body, divide the joint at 5. The neck bones are freed the same as in a turkey. The breast of a goose is considered the most choice part, though all of the meat is good, and full of juicy flavor.

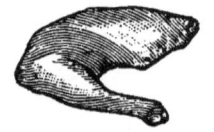

Fig. 18.

The leg, wing and neck bone are shown above (Fig. 18).

Roast Duck.

No other dishes require so much skill in carving as game and poultry; as it is necessary to be well acquainted with the anatomy of the bird in order to place the knife at exactly the right point. A young duckling may be carved, by first taking off the legs and wings, but if it is very small, it will be as well not to separate them, as they will both be needed for a single portion in serving. When the duck is large, carve it like a goose, by cutting pieces from the breast, beginning close to the wing and proceeding upward toward the breast-bone.

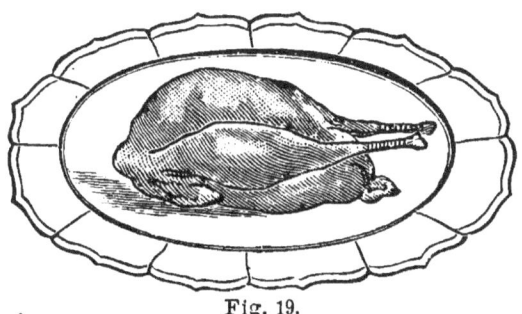

Fig. 19.

If there is not enough meat on the breast to supply all the guests, the legs and wings must be used. The wing of a flyer and the leg of a swimmer are the most desirable portions of a duck. Some are fond of the feet, and in dressing the duck these should be skinned and never removed.

Roast Rabbit.

Draw the knife the whole length of the backbone, as shown by the dotted line 3 to 4, dividing the body first into two parts. Remove the leg as shown by the line 5 to 6, and

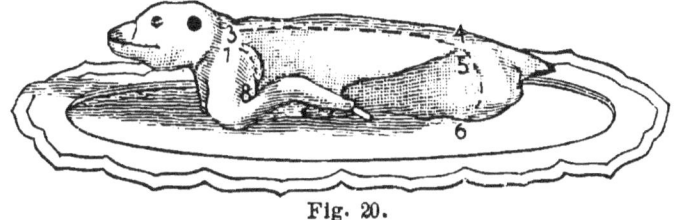

Fig. 20.

20   THE KITCHEN.

the shoulder as indicated by the one from 7 to 8. Next, cu
off the head and the ears close to the roots, and divide the
upper from the lower jaw. Put the point of the knife into
the forehead and divide it through the centre down to the
nose. Cut the back into several pieces if large, into only two
if small, and serve each guest, with dressing and gravy, to
such parts as are preferred.

Roast Partridge.

There are several ways of carving this most familiar game-
bird. The usual method is to carry the knife along the top of
the breast-bone and cut it quite through, dividing it into two
equal parts. Another mode is to cut it in three pieces, by sev-

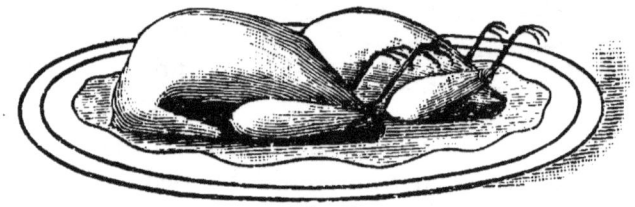

Fig. 21.

ering a small wing and leg on either side from the body, thus
making two helpings of these parts, and one of the breast for
a third plate. The third mode is to thrust back the body from
the legs, and then cut through the middle of the breast, so as
to give four or more small helpings.

Boiled Salmon.

First run the knife down to the bone along the side of the fish from 9 to 10, also from 3 to 4. Help the thick part length- wise, that is, in the

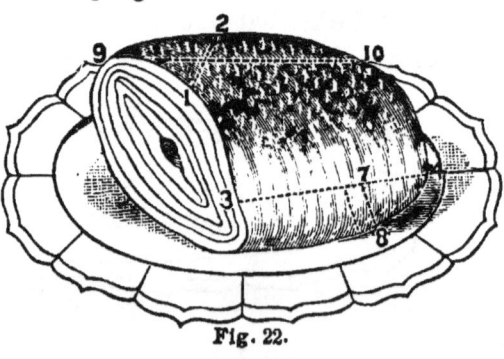

Fig. 22.

About Carving.

direction of the line from 9 to 10, and the thin part, breadthwise, or in the direction of 7 to 8. A slice of the thick part with one of the thin, where lies the fat, should be served to each guest. Care should be taken, in serving, not to break the flakes and thus impair its beauty.

Cod's Head and Shoulders.

Pass the fish slice in the direction of 2 to 5, down to the bone; then help pieces between 1 and 6, or from the opposite side and serve some of the sound with each slice. This lies under the backbone, and is obtained by passing the knife in the direction of 2 to 5. The oyster, or cheek below the eye, is a delicate part, as are the tongue and palate. To get at these, pass the slice or spoon into the mouth.

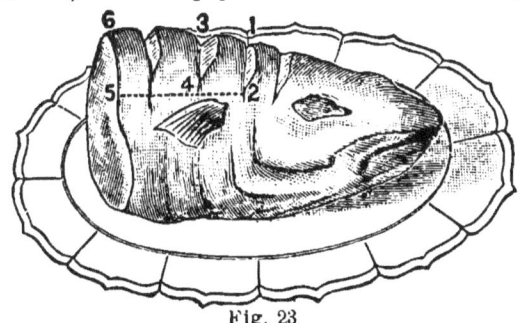
Fig. 23

Mackerel.

The head and tail may be first removed by passing the slice downward from 1 and 2; they should then be split down the back, so as to serve each person to a side; or, if less is required, the thickest part should be given. The roe, which many esteem, will be found between 1 and 2.

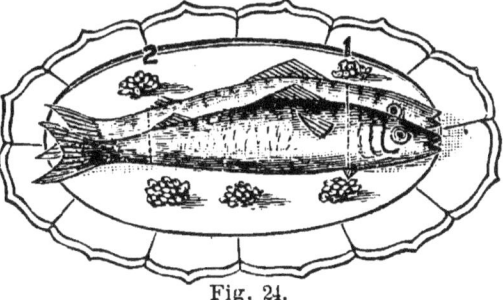
Fig. 24.

SOUPS.

Beef Stock.

To make this merely for the stock, get a knuckle of beef and separate the beef from the bones, cutting it into small pieces. Break the bones also, and add to this 1 quart of water for each pound of meat. When it begins to boil, remove the scum, being careful to do this so long as it rises. Set the soup kettle where it will simmer for 5 or 6 hours, or until the substance of the meat is thoroughly extracted. Then add salt sufficient to season it, and skim out the meat. Strain the liquid, and put it away to cool and for the fat to rise. When entirely cold, remove the fat and there will remain a firm, gelatinous mass, which can be used in soups, gravies, etc.

Beef Soup.

Put into beef stock made as above, 3 carrots, 2 turnips, 2 onions, 1 head of celery, cut into small pieces; a little thyme, salt and pepper to taste, and simmer slowly until the vegetables are done. Serve at once.

Chicken Soup.

Boil a pair of chickens with great care, skimming constantly, keeping them covered with water. When tender, take out the chicken and remove the bones. Put a large lump of butter into a spider, dredge the chicken-meat well with flour, and lay in the hot pan; fry a nice brown, and keep hot and dry. Stir into 1 pint of the chicken water 2 large spoonfuls of curry powder, 2 of butter, 1 of flour, 1 teaspoonful of salt and a little cayenne; then mix it with the broth in the pot. Simmer five minutes, add the browned chicken, and serve.

Celery Soup.

Make a good broth of a shank of beef, skim off the fat, and thicken the broth with a little flour mixed with water. Cut into small pieces 1 large bunch of celery, or 2 small ones; boil them in the soup till tender. Add 1 cup of rich cream, with pepper and salt.

Bean Soup.

The small white field beans are preferable. Put them to soak the evening before in cold water. In the morning set them on to boil in the soaking water, or enough of it to keep them cooking well, without burning. Boil slowly until they have all bursted, then add them to the meat designed for the soup. A shin of beef, cut into small pieces, is good for this purpose. Add 1 quart of water for each pound of meat. One must watch this last process carefully, or the beans will burn. Put some small pieces of toasted bread into a soup tureen, and pour the soup over it. Split pea soup may be made in the same way as the above.

Beef Tea.

Cut 1 pound of perfectly lean beef into small pieces, half an inch square; put them into a wide-mouthed jar, and cork tightly. Set the jar into a kettle of cold water placed on the stove where it will heat gradually until it boils. Keep it boiling an hour. Take out the jar, and, when cooled a little, strain the juice through a piece of coarse linen. Add no water or seasoning excepting a small pinch of salt.

Tomato Soup.

To 1 pint tomatoes canned, or 4 large raw ones, cut up fine, add 1 quart boiling water, and let them boil. Then add

1 teaspoonful of soda, 1 pint of sweet milk, with salt, pepper and plenty of butter. When this boils, add 8 small crackers rolled fine.

Ox-Tail Soup.

Cut 2 ox-tails up at the joints, wash and put them in a kettle with 1 ounce of butter and ½ pint of water. Stir it over the fire till the juices are drawn, adding 2 carrots, 2 turnips, 3 onions, 1 leek, 1 head of celery, 1 bunch of savory herbs, 1 bay leaf, 12 peppercorns, 4 cloves. Cut the vegetables in slices, and pour over all 3 quarts of water and one tablespoonful salt. Skim well and simmer very gently 3 or 4 hours, or until tender. Take out the tails, strain the soup, thicken with flour, and add 2 tablespoonfuls catsup and ⅓ glass of port wine. Put back the tails, simmer for 5 minutes, and serve.

Soup a la Reine.

Take the white meat of cold roast chicken and pound it with ½ teacupful of slightly cooked rice. When well pounded, dilute with 1 quart of stock, strain through a sieve, and add salt and pepper to taste. Heat it, and serve. If stock is not at hand, put the chicken bones over to cook, with an onion, a blade of mace, a carrot, a few sweet herbs, salt and pepper, and stew 3 hours.

Mock Turtle Soup.

Scald a calf's head with the skin on, remove the brain, tie the head up in a cloth, and let it boil for 1 hour. Then take the meat from the bones, cut it into small square pieces, and throw it into cold water. When cool, put it into a stew-pan and cover with 3 quarts of stock; let it boil an hour or more, then set it aside; melt ¼ pound of butter in another stew-pan and add ¼ pound of ham cut small, 2 tablespoonfuls minced parsley, 2 onions, a few chopped mushrooms and nearly a pint

Soups. 25

of stock; let these simmer slowly for 2 hours and then dredge in flour to dry up the butter. Add the rest of the stock and ¼ bottle of Madeira or sherry; let it stew gently for 10 minutes; rub it through a soup sieve. Put it to the calf's head; season with cayenne, and, if requisite, a little salt; add the juice of an orange and lemon, and, if liked, ¼ teaspoonful of pounded mace. Put in forcemeat balls, simmer 5 minutes; serve hot.

Egg Soup.

Beat a tablespoonful of flour in a teaspoonful of cold stock, and put in 4 eggs; throw them into boiling stock, stirring all of the time. Add 2 small blades of mace. Boil 15 minutes. Season, and serve with a French roll in the tureen, or with small bits of bread.

Corn Soup.

To 1 can of sweet corn take 1 quart each of milk and water. Season with salt, pepper, 2 tablespoonfuls butter and 1 tablespoonful of flour. Boil 10 or 15 minutes. Add 2 or 3 well-beaten eggs and ½ teacupful cracker crumbs.

Asparagus Soup.

To 50 heads of asparagus take 1 quart of stock. Boil the asparagus in 1 pint water until the heads are nearly done. Drain the asparagus, cut off the green heads, and put them aside until the soup is ready. Boil the stems a little longer in the stock, add the asparagus water, and when it boils, drop in the green heads—or peas, as they are called—and simmer 2 or 3 minutes. After the soup is put into the tureen, a small quantity of sherry added to it improves it.

Julienne Soup.

Shred 2 onions, and fry brown in a ½ spoonful of butter; add a little mace, salt and pepper; then a spoonful or so of stock ; rub a tablespoonful of flour smooth with a little butter, and let fry with the onions; strain through a colander, then add more stock as desired; cut turnip, carrot and celery in fillets; add a few green peas; boil tender in a little water, and add both water and vegetables to the soup. The flour can be left out, and it will make a clear, light-colored soup. In that case the onions should be cut in fillets and boiled with the vegetables.

Oyster Soup.

Pour 1 quart of boiling water into a kettle ; then 1 quart of good rich milk ; stir in 1 teacupful of rolled cracker crumbs, seasoned with pepper and salt to taste. When all come to a boil, add 1 quart of good fresh oysters; stir well, so as to keep from scorching; lastly add a piece of sweet butter, about the size of an egg ; let it boil up once ; then remove from the fire immediately ; dish up and send to table.

Noodle Soup.

Use either fresh beef or mutton. Allow a quart of water to each pound of meat, exclusive of the bones. When the scum no longer rises, add carrots, turnips and onions cut in small pieces, and boil until very tender. Remove the meat and strain the soup. Add a large quantity of the "noodles," made thus : Mix into pastry, flour, beaten eggs and a little butter. Roll this very thin, fold it up closely; cut it into strings like cutting cabbage for cold "slaw." Throw this into the soup, and boil 10 to 15 minutes.

FISH.

Fish are considered in best condition just before the spawning season, and unfit for use when it is just over. The flesh will then assume a bluish tinge when boiled, but when in season it will boil white and curdy. It is a common error to wash fish too much, as thus its flavor is greatly impaired. It can be wiped very clean with a soft cloth, using scarcely any

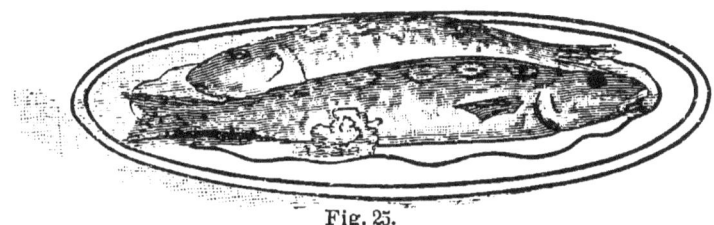

Fig. 25.

water. For fish to be boiled, it is well to put a little salt and vinegar into the water after it is cleaned, to give firmness to the flesh. It should be put into cold water and set on the fire, where it will cook gently, or the skin will break before the inside is done.

The carver should avoid the use of steel knives, and, if possible, serve with a silver fish slice. He should also serve each one to a piece of the choicest parts.

Cod's Head and Shoulders.

Cleanse the fish thoroughly, and rub a little salt over the thick part and inside of the fish one or two hours before dressing it, as this very much improves the flavor. Lay it in a fish-kettle, with sufficient cold water to cover it; do not pour the water on the fish, as it is liable to break it. If the water boils away, add a little by pouring it in at the sides of the kettle. Add 5 ounces of salt to each gallon of water, and bring it gradually to a boil. Skim very carefully, and let it gently simmer till done, then take it out and drain. Place on a hot napkin, and garnish with lemon and horse-radish. Oyster sauce and plain melted butter may be served with this.

Boiled Salmon.

Scale and clean the fish, being careful to remove all the blood ; lay it in the fish-kettle, with salted water sufficient to cover it. Let it boil slowly, removing the scum as it rises. When it is done, which will be when the meat separates easily from the bone, take it from the kettle, drain it, and serve on a napkin with slices of lemon and parsley as a garnish. Send lobster or shrimp sauce and plain melted butter to table with it. A dish of dressed cucumber usually accompanies this dish.

Fried Smelts, or Brochet of Smelts.

Smelts should be very fresh, and not washed more than is necessary. Dry them in a cloth, and season with a little salt and pepper ; then dip them in beaten egg, and roll in fine cracker crumbs. Drop them in hot lard, and fry to a delicate

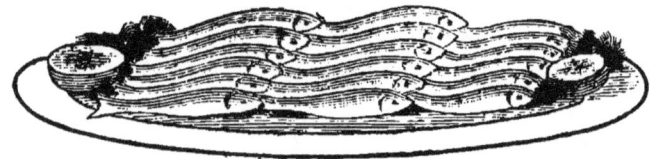

Fig. 26.

brown. Drain them on soft paper, being careful not to remove the light roughness of the crumbs. Arrange them on short skewers, as shown in Fig. 26, on a hot napkin, and garnish with lemon and curled parsley.

Baked Salmon Trout, with Cream Gravy.

Clean the fish carefully, wipe it dry and lay in the baking-pan, salting and peppering it a little, and adding very little water. Baste it frequently with butter and water. When it is done, have ready a gravy made of a cup of cream, thinned with three or four tablespoonfuls hot water. Stir into this two tablespoonfuls melted butter and a little minced parsley. Put it on to scald in a farina boiler, and stir into it a little thickening ; also add to it the gravy from the baked fish Lay the trout on a platter and pour the gravy over it. Garnish with parsley and sliced lemon.

Sun Fish.

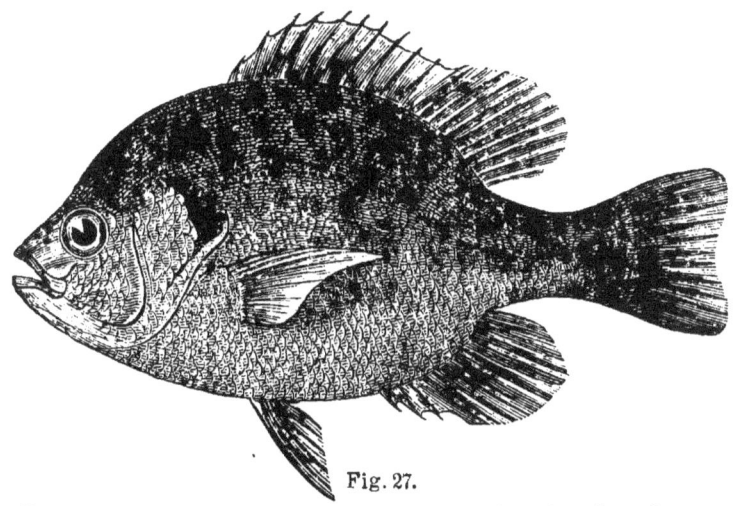

Fig. 27.

This fish is doubtless so named from its circular form and shining surface. It is an excellent pan fish. Roll in cracker crumbs, fry a golden brown ; season with salt and pepper.

Baked Shad.

Thoroughly clean the shad, leaving the head on, as it looks much better when sent to the table. Wipe it very dry, have it opened on the belly, stuff it with bread crumbs seasoned with cream or butter, and a little milk, salt, pepper, and a sprig of thyme, or, if preferred, a little chopped onion. Sew it up carefully, put it in the dripping-pan, with very little water. Baste it occasionally with salted water and butter. Bake an hour, and serve with caper sauce.

Sheepshead.

This excellent fish is found along the whole Atlantic coast to as far north as Cape Cod. It is so named from the resemblance of its profile and teeth to those of a sheep. Its habits

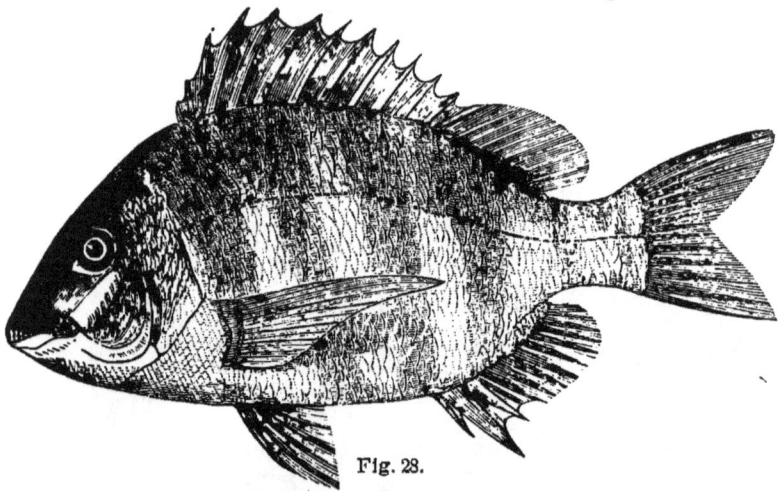

Fig. 28.

are also suggestive of the same animal, as it feeds with a grazing motion upon barnacles and shells. It may be fried or broiled, as best suits one's tastes.

Forcemeat Balls, for Fish Soups.

One middling-sized lobster, ¼ an anchovy, one head of boiled celery, the yolk of a hard-boiled egg, salt, cayenne, and mace to taste ; 4 tablespoonfuls of bread crumbs, 2 ounces of

FISH. 31

butter, 2 eggs. Pick the meat from the shell of the lobster and pound it with the soft parts in a mortar; add the celery, the yolk of the egg, seasoning and bread crumbs. Mix the whole thoroughly either in a mortar or by kneading. Warm the butter and beat the eggs well, and amalgamate them with the pounded lobster meat. Make the balls about an inch in diameter, and fry a nice brown. Eighteen or twenty of these suffice for one tureen of soup.

Spanish Mackerel.

This popular fish is rarely found north of Cape Cod, as it prefers a warm climate; but they are abundant on the Gulf coast of Florida, and at various other points on the Gulf. Open

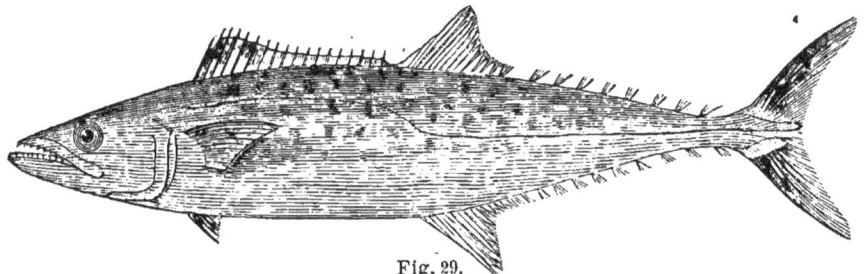

Fig. 29.

them on the back, and broil over a clear fire, avoiding scorching, as the delicate flavor is easily impaired. Season with butter, pepper and salt to taste. Serve at once.

Scalloped Fish.

Pick any cold fish carefully from the bones, and moisten with milk and an egg. Place in a deep dish the fish with bread crumbs, a teaspoonful of anchovy sauce, 1 blade pounded mace, 2 tablespoonfuls butter, and salt to taste. Put the crumbs on the top, with butter, and brown in the oven. Serve very hot.

BEEF.

Roast Beef.

A piece of beef weighing 8 or 10 pounds will take a little over 2 hours to roast. Some allow 15 minutes to each pound of beef. Prepare it by wiping with a dry napkin, but never washing, rub over it a little salt and pepper, and put it into a *dry* pan to roast in a hot oven. The heat will soon seal in the juices and retain them till the piece is cut at the table. Baste occasionally. If the flavor of sweet herbs and vegetables (as carrot, turnip, onion, etc.) is relished in the gravy, put a few slices of these last, with a bay leaf or two and a little thyme and parsley, into the pan, to make a bed on which to lay the beef. When it is done, add more seasoning, remove the beef, take out the vegetables if used, add hot water to the gravy, thicken it, being careful to avoid lumps. Serve either over the meat or in a gravy-boat, as one prefers.

Beefsteak.

Select choice steaks, from ¾ of an inch to 1 inch thick; trim off all superfluous fat and bone. Broil on a wire gridiron, over a clear but not too hot fire. Watch it carefully, to avoid scorching. When browned nicely, remove to a platter, season with pepper, salt, and a pretty liberal supply of butter. No definite rule can be given as to the *time* of cooking steak, individual tastes differ so widely in regard to it, some only liking it when well done, others so rare that the blood runs out of it.

A La Mode Beef.

Take a piece of beef four or five inches thick, and with a small knife make little holes entirely through it at small distances apart. Then roll strips of fat salt pork in pepper and cloves and draw them into these openings; lay on a pan, cover closely, put in a steamer, and steam for three hours. When done, thicken the gravy with a little flour. This is excellent eaten as cold meat.

Staffordshire Beefsteak.

Beat the steaks a little with a rolling-pin, flour and season, then fry with a sliced onion to a fine light brown ; lay them into a stew-pan, and pour as much boiling water over them as will serve for sauce ; stew them very gently half an hour, and add a spoonful of catsup before serving.

Pressed Beef.

Select any kind of lean beef, as the shoulder clod or the upper part of round beef, next to the soup pieces. Cut it into small pieces and put over it enough cold water to come up around it. Cover the kettle closely, so as to keep in all the steam. Cook slowly until it will all fall to pieces, which takes several hours. It must be watched, to avoid boiling away or scorching. There should be less than a teacupful of liquor to four pounds of meat. Skim off all the fat from the top. While hot, stir in this liquor a good sized teaspoonful of gelatine. After removing all the bones and fat from the meat, chop it fine while hot. Then put it in the dish for pressing. Pour over the liquor, stir it up well, add salt to taste, and pepper also, if one likes it. Then turn a plate over it, put on a heavy weight, and let it stand a few hours to harden.

Roast Beef, with Yorkshire Pudding.

Put the meat in a hot oven, after dredging it with flour. Baste it frequently. Half an hour before it is done, put it over the pudding made thus : Put 6 large tablespoonfuls flour into a basin with a little salt, and stir gradually into this $1\frac{1}{2}$

pints milk and 3 eggs. Beat the mixture for a few minutes, pour it into a shallow, buttered tin, bake it for an hour, and, for another half hour, place it under the meat to catch a little of the gravy that flows from it. Cut the pudding into small square pieces, put them on a hot dish, and serve. The beef, for this purpose, should rest upon a small three-cornered stand.

Corned Beef.

Put it into cold water to cook, and keep it well covered till very tender. Let it cool in the liquor, unless it is to be eaten hot. Take out the bones, and press in a mould or on a plate.

Fried Beef's Liver.

Cut rather thin, and pour boiling water over it; drain perfectly. Roll the liver in fine bread crumbs, season with salt and pepper, and fry quickly in hot fat to a crisp brown.

Boiled Beef's Tongue.

Boil in plenty of water till very tender. If a salt tongue is used, either soak it in water over night before cooking, or pour off the first water in boiling. While warm, remove the skin.

Boiled Tongue, with Tomato Sauce.

Half boil a tongue, then stew it with a sauce made of a little broth, flour, parsley, 1 small onion, 1 small carrot, salt and pepper, and 1 can of tomatoes cooked and strained. Lay the tongue on a dish and strain the sauce over it.

Mince Meat.

Boil 3 pounds of lean beef until very tender, then chop fine. Mix with this, 1 pound beef suet, fine.; 5 pounds apples, 2 pounds raisins, 2 pounds currants, 2 tablespoonfuls cinnamon, 1 tablespoonful each of mace and cloves, 1 nutmeg, grated; ½ tablespoonful allspice— all the spices ground; 1 tea-

BEEF. 35

spoonful salt, 2¼ pounds sugar, a quart of sweet cider, and 1 pint of brandy. Have the cider boiling hot, and the brandy cold, when added. If this is followed exactly, and the mince meat kept in a cool place, it will keep all winter. It should stand a day or two after mixing before it is used.

Curried Beef.

A few slices of tolerably lean cold roast or boiled beef, 3 ounces of butter, 2 onions, 1 wineglass of beer, 1 dessert spoonful of curry powder. Cut the beef into pieces about an inch square. Put the butter into a stew-pan, and fry the onions to a light brown. Add the other ingredients, and stir gently over a brisk fire about 10 minutes. Should this be thought too dry, more beer, or a little gravy or water, may be added, but a good curry should not be very thin. Place it in a deep dish, with an edging of boiled rice, the same as for other curries.

Beef Kidney, to Dress.

Cut the kidneys into neat slices, soak them in warm water 2 hours, changing it two or three times; then dry them on a clean cloth and fry to a nice brown in butter. Season each side with pepper and salt and pour over them a highly seasoned gravy in which has been mixed 1 tablespoonful lemon juice and ¼ teaspoonful powdered sugar.

Beef Rissoles.

To each pound of cold roast beef allow ¾ pound of bread crumbs, salt and pepper to taste, a few chopped savory herbs, ½ a teaspoonful minced lemon-peel, 2 eggs. To the meat, minced fine, add the bread crumbs, seasoning, lemon-peel and eggs in the above proportion. Make all into a thick paste; divide into balls or cones, and fry a rich brown. Garnish with parsley, and serve either with or without a brown gravy, as preferred.

VEAL.

Roast Veal.

Select meat that is firm and the fat white. The loin is one of the most desirable parts for roasting. Rub it well with salt and a little pepper. Either with or without a larding needle, draw in bits of salt pork to give it richness. Make a dressing of bread crumbs, well seasoned and moistened with milk or water. Fasten this in under the loin securely, and put into a hot oven to bake. Baste it frequently, and when well done, take up; thicken the gravy, and serve. The same herbs and vegetables that are used for roasting beef may be put under the veal if preferred.

Minced Veal.

Take 3 pounds of uncooked veal, chop fine; add 3 beaten eggs, butter the size of an egg, 4 rolled crackers, and enough pepper and salt to season well; $\frac{1}{2}$ grated nutmeg; mix. Press it into a crock or earthen dish, and bake half an hour. When ready to serve, turn it out and slice down on a platter. Beef is good prepared in the same manner.

Fricandeau of Veal.

Choose a thick piece of veal from the leg, weighing three or four pounds, and lard it thus: Cut from very firm salt pork, pieces $\frac{1}{2}$ of an inch thick and 3 or 4 inches long. With the sharp point of a knife, make incisions in the upper part of the veal; draw into each of these a strip of the pork. Continue this process until the whole top is covered with the larding. Let every alternate strip lie in a different direction, so as to give an ornamental finish to the top. Put into the

Veal Croquettes.

Take very fine minced veal, moisten with cream and a beaten egg; season with salt, sweet marjoram and a little pounded mace; form into small cones either by hand or in a wine glass; crumb the outside, and fry, or else set in the oven and bake, basting frequently.

Veal Cutlets and Olives.

This is very pretty for a luncheon or supper dish, and also appropriate for an *entrée*. Prepare the cutlets by cutting them in oval form two or three inches wide, a little longer, and half

Fig. 30.

an inch thick. Dip them in egg, then in fine cracker crumbs, and repeat this until they are thoroughly encrusted; then fry them carefully in butter. Arrange them on the platter, as shown above. Garnish with olives.

Veal Collops.

Cut veal from the leg or other lean part into pieces the size of an oyster. Season with pepper, salt and a little mace; rub some over each piece; dip in egg, then into cracker crumbs, and fry. They both look and taste like oysters.

oven and bake; when the juices are sealed in, or in half an hour, season it with salt and pepper. Do not let it scorch. When done, make a gravy as for roast veal.

Boiled Calf's Head (with the Skin on).

Put the head into boiling water and let it remain 3 or 4 minutes; take it out, hold it by the ear, and (with the back of the knife) scrape off all the hair. When clean, take out the eyes, cut off the ears, and remove the brains, which soak for an hour in warm water. Put the head into hot water for a few minutes, to make it look white, then lay it in a stew-pan, and gradually bring it to boil. Simmer it very gently from 2½ to 3 hours; when nearly done, boil the brains ¼ hour. Skin and chop them, not too finely, adding a tablespoonful of minced, scalded parsley. Season with pepper and salt, and stir the brains, parsley, etc., into 4 tablespoonfuls of melted butter; add 1 tablespoonful of lemon juice, 2 or 3 grains of cayenne, and keep these hot by the fire. Take up the head, cut out the tongue, skin it, put it on a small dish with the brains round it; sprinkle bread crumbs over the head; brown it in the oven, and serve with a tureen of parsley and butter, and either boiled ham, bacon, or pickled pork, as an accompaniment.

Boiled Calf's Feet and Parsley and Butter.

Take 2 white calves' feet; bone them as far as the first joint, and soak 2 hours in warm water. Put them in a saucepan, with 2 slices of bacon, 2 ounces butter, 2 tablespoonfuls lemon juice, salt and pepper to taste, 1 onion, a bunch of savory herbs, 4 cloves, 1 blade of mace, a little minced parsley, and water enough to cover the whole. Stew slowly for about 3 hours, then take out the feet, dish them, and cover with parsley and butter. The liquor they were boiled in should be strained and put by for use; it will be found very good as an addition to gravies.

PORK.

Boiled Ham.

Soak in water a few hours, and put on to boil in enough cold water to cover it; cook slowly till tender. Let it remain in the kettle to cool, and take off the skin and smoky parts. Dust it with cracker crumbs, having first coated it with egg. Put it into the oven and let it bake slowly for an hour.

Broiled Ham.

The thickness of the slices must depend upon individual tastes, some liking it very thin, others the reverse. Have a clear fire, not too hot. So soon as partially browned, dip it into cold water and return to the gridiron; repeat this process twice, unless the ham is very fresh. Then finish it carefully, butter and send to the table hot.

Ham Omelet.

Take 6 eggs, 4 ounces butter, a pinch of pepper, 2 tablespoonfuls ham. Mince the ham very fine, and fry it 2 minutes in a little butter; then make the batter for the omelet; stir in the ham, and proceed as in the case of a plain omelet. Do not add salt to the batter, as the ham seasons it sufficiently. Good lean bacon or tongue answers equally well for this dish.

Ham and Eggs.

Fry the ham quickly, having previously soaked it for a little while in cold water. Place on a platter. Drop into this hot fat, eggs from a saucer, so as not to break them. Let them cook slowly, by dipping the hot fat over them. Lay each one, as done, on the slices of ham. Garnish with parsley, and serve at once.

MUTTON.

Spring Lamb, with Mint Sauce.

Select a quarter of lamb that is fat, and has not been too recently killed. Season it well by rubbing salt on all parts thoroughly. Roast till tender, basting it with the drippings. For the mint sauce, strip the leaves from spearmint, chop them very fine, add a little salt, a large spoonful powdered sugar and a cupful of vinegar. Pour the vinegar over the mint sometime before it is to be served, so as to draw out the strength. Serve this with the lamb, which may be garnished with curled parsley and lemon.

Lamb Chops.

A pyramid of gold-browned mashed potatoes with a border of lamb chops, makes a pretty *entrée*. Trim the chops well

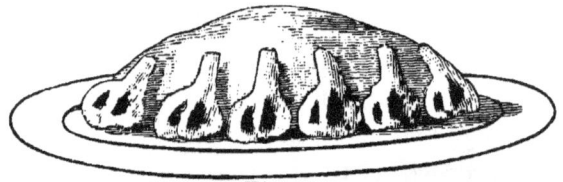

Fig. 31.

before cooking, leaving only a thin border of fat around the edge; fry in hot lard to a nice color. Arrange them around the potato centre, as seen above.

Boiled Leg of Lamb.

Choose a joint weighing about 5 pounds. Plunge it into a kettle of boiling water to seal in the juices; when it boils up again, draw it from the fire and let it cook slowly 1¼ hours, or until tender. Make a white sauce, dish the lamb and pour

MUTTON. 41

it over it, garnishing with tufts of cauliflower or carrots. Send to the table some of the sauce in a tureen.

Boiled Mutton, with Caper Sauce.

Boil a leg of mutton in plenty of water, 2 to 3 hours, depending upon the weight of the piece. Make a sauce of milk or water, as preferred, adding butter, pepper, salt, and two tablespoonfuls caper sauce. Some put a little vinegar in the water in which the mutton is boiled, if not very young.

Saddle of Mutton.

To prepare this handsome *entrée*, remove all the bones carefully without injury to the skin on the upper side. Fill this cavity with dressing, and roll the whole up in a buttered cloth, tying with a string. Stew 1½ hours in white stock, with

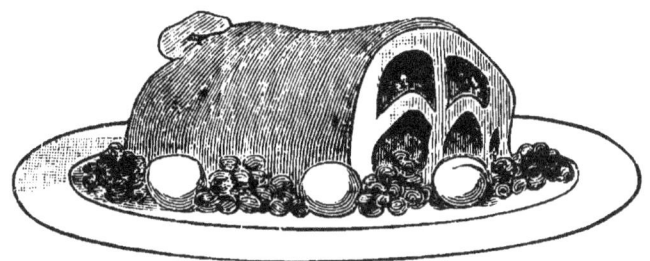

Fig. 32.

the usual amount of stock vegetables. Then press it between two plates until cold. Before serving, make it hot (but do not boil it) in a little of the stock, place it on a dish, as seen in Fig. 32, garnish with button mushrooms, truffles and lemons. Pour Allemande or any good cold sauce over the meat.

Mutton Stew.

Take pieces of mutton unfit for cutlets, cover with water; add a little onion and parsley, and season well with pepper and salt. Cook slowly until the meat is very tender. Thicken the gravy with flour and the grated yolks of 2 hard-boiled eggs. Serve as soon as it boils up.

Mutton Collops.

Cut some very thin slices from the leg or the thick end of a loin of mutton, sprinkle with pepper, salt, pounded mace, savory herbs, and a little chopped onion; fry them in butter, stir in a dessert spoonful of flour, add ½ pint gravy and a little lemon juice. Simmer gently about 5 minutes, and serve.

Broiled Mutton, with Tomato Sauce.

Cut slices from a leg or a shoulder of mutton, broil them quickly over a clear fire, and season with pepper and salt. Make some tomato sauce by cooking and straining it through a colander, and adding butter, salt, pepper and a little cracker dust. Pour it over the mutton, and serve very hot.

Lamb Cutlets and Green Peas.

Trim lamb cutlets carefully, leaving the ends bare for an inch or more, making them about ¼ of an inch in thickness. Broil over a clear fire to a nice brown. Season with butter,

Fig. 33.

pepper and salt. Allow two cutlets to each person. Arrange on a platter, as shown in Fig. 33, with a bed of green peas around them. Either asparagus or spinach may be used instead of the peas.

POULTRY.

Select young fowls—plump, white, and not overfed. If their legs are smooth, and the cartilage soft at the end of the breast-bone, they are young. For boiling, white-legged ones are preferred, as the meat is whiter; but for roasting, the darker-legged varieties are thought to be more juicy.

Croquettes of Fowl.

Mince together the dark and white meat from a cold fowl. Put it into a saucepan with some of the liquor in which the chicken was boiled. Add a tablespoonful of cream, and a little salt and pepper, thicken it with flour. Let it come to a boil, and pour it into a dish. When cool, make it into rolls or

Fig. 34.

small conical shapes. Roll each in fine cracker or bread crumbs, then in well-beaten eggs, and again in the crumbs. Have ready a kettle of hot lard, drop them in, and cook to a light brown. Arrange them on a napkin in a dish as shown above. Garnish with curled parsley.

Broiled Chicken.

For broiling, young chickens should be chosen, and carefully dressed. Cut them open on the back, laying them out as flat as possible. Cut off the first joint of the wings and neck, and cook them with the giblets. Have a clear, but not too hot fire, over which to broil them. Watch carefully, so as to have every part nicely browned, but not scorched. Take up on a hot platter, season with pepper and salt, and a liberal supply of butter. Chop the giblets, with the little meat from the neck and wing-tips ; thicken, and serve, either by pouring over the chicken, or in a gravy tureen.

Roasted Chicken.

Select a good-sized, plump, but not too fat, chicken ; pluck it carefully, and wash in cold water. Make a dressing of bread crumbs, with a little butter, salt, pepper, thyme, and 1 or 2 eggs. Soften it with milk or water. Fill the fowl with the dressing, sew up, skewer well, and put it in the pan to bake. Baste frequently with butter and water, and turn it occasionally. If it browns too fast, cover the exposed parts with buttered paper. When done, remove from the oven, and keep hot till the gravy is made ready. The giblets should be cooked and chopped while the chicken is roasting, and put into the gravy after the thickening has been added. Serve at once.

Curried Chicken.

Slice 2 large onions ; peel, core, and chop an apple, and cut the fowl into joints; fry these brown in 2 ounces of butter, then add a dessert-spoonful of curry powder, $\frac{1}{2}$ pint of gravy, a teaspoonful flour, and stir for about 20 minutes. Put in 1 tablespoonful lemon juice, and serve with boiled rice, either placed in a ridge around the dish, or separately.

Pressed Chicken.

Cook three or four chickens in a little water, until very tender, so that the flesh will readily separate from the bones.

POULTRY. 45

Season the whole. Then take out the meat and pick it up fine, removing the skin, and mixing the white and dark meats together. Add to the liquor in which they were boiled a tablespoonful of cooking gelatine for each three or four pounds of chicken. Place the chicken in a mould, or earthen dish, and pour the liquor over it while hot. Stir it up well, then turn a plate over it, put on a heavy weight, and set it away to cool.

Chicken Pie.

Prepare the chicken as for stewing, and cook until it begins to get tender. Cover the bottom of a basin with peeled potatoes partly cooked, putting them in with the chicken; make the crust of 1 pint of buttermilk, 1 even teaspoonful soda, butter about the size of a hen's egg, a pinch of salt, and flour enough to roll well. Merely line the sides of the pan with crust. Thicken the gravy, and pour it over the chicken, season with butter, pepper and salt. Cover the top with crust about one-half inch thick. Bake 30 minutes in a moderately hot oven.

Potted Chicken. (A Luncheon or Breakfast Dish.)

Strip the meat from the bones of a cold roast fowl; to every pound of meat allow $\frac{1}{4}$ pound of butter, salt and cayenne to taste; 1 teaspoonful pounded mace, $\frac{1}{2}$ small nutmeg. Cut the meat into small pieces, pound it well with the butter, sprinkle in the spices gradually, and keep pounding until reduced to a perfectly smooth paste. Put it into small jars, and cover with clarified butter, about $\frac{1}{4}$ of an inch in thickness. Two or three slices of ham, minced and pounded with the above, will be an improvement. Keep in a dry place.

Roast Goose.

Select a goose with a clean white skin, plump breast and yellow feet; if these latter are red, the bird is old. Hanging a few days improves the flavor. Pluck, singe, draw and carefully wash and wipe the goose; cut off the neck close to the back, leaving the skin long enough to turn over; cut off the feet, and beat the breast bone flat. Put a skewer through the under part of each wing, draw up the legs closely, put a skewer into the middle of each and pass it through the body. Make a stuffing of bread crumbs, onions, sage, butter, salt and pepper to taste; put it into the body of the goose and secure it firmly. Roast in a hot oven from 1½ to 2 hours, according to size, keeping it well basted. Remove the skewers, serve with a tureen of good gravy and one of apple sauce.

Roast Ducks.

Ducks may be trussed with the feet on, which should be scalded, the skin peeled off, and then turned up close to the legs. Draw the legs as closely as possible to the body, to plump up the breast, passing the skewer quite through the body. If cooking a pair, make a stuffing of sage and onion sufficient for one duck, and leave the other unseasoned, as the flavor is not liked by every one. Put them in a hot oven to roast, and baste very often. Send them to the table with a good brown gravy poured round but *not over* them, and a little of the same in a tureen. When in season, green peas should accompany this dish.

TURKEYS.

Young cock turkeys may be known by their short spurs and black legs; if the spurs are long and the legs rough, they are old; if the eyes are dull and the feet dry the bird has been long killed. They should never be dressed the same day they are killed; if the weather will admit of it they should hang from three to seven days before picking, as this will greatly improve their flavor and quality.

Roast Turkey.

Have the turkey well picked, washed and thoroughly dried. Prepare a stuffing of bread crumbs, butter, summer savory or sweet thyme, pepper and salt to taste, and some prefer a little onion chopped very fine. Fill the breast and body with the stuffing, sew up the openings, truss it, and put it in the pan to roast. It requires frequent basting. When done, make a brown gravy and add the chopped giblets, which should be boiled tender in advance. Fried sausages make a pretty garnish for roast turkey, and some like the flavor of a little chopped sausage in the dressing.

Boiled Turkey.

Prepare the fowl the same as for roasting, and make a stuffing of bread crumbs mixed with cream or butter, oysters and the yolks of eggs. Fill the bird, sew it in, truss it, and place it in sufficient boiling water to cover it well. Let it cook slowly for two hours, more or less, depending upon its size. Skim it well while boiling. Serve it with celery sauce or with drawn butter and oysters.

Force-meat for Veal, Turkeys, Fowls, etc.

Take 2 ounces of ham or lean bacon, ¼ pound of suet, and the rind of ½ a lemon, 1 teaspoonful each of minced parsley and sweet herbs ; salt, cayenne and pounded mace to taste ; 6 ounces of bread crumbs, 2 eggs. Shred the ham or bacon, chop the suet, lemon peel and herbs, taking great care that all be finely minced ; add a seasoning to taste of salt, cayenne and mace, and blend all thoroughly together with the bread crumbs before wetting. Beat the eggs, and work them up with the other ingredients, and the force-meat will be ready for use. Either fry the balls in hot lard, or put them on a tin and bake ½ an hour in a moderate oven.

GAME.

Game, as woodcock, partridge, snipe, etc., should not be plucked until a day or two after they are killed; and, if the weather will allow, they are better flavored for hanging 3 or 4

Fig. 35. 1. Snipe; 2. Quail.

days in a cool place before cooking. The tastes of the guests vary as to the time of keeping; and what would be delicious to some, would be wholly unpalatable to others.

Roast Snipe.

Pluck and wipe the birds on the outside. They are said to be best without drawing; but one's taste must govern in the matter. Skin the head and neck, and truss them with the head under the wing. Twist the legs at the first joint, press the feet upon the thighs, and pass a skewer through these and the body. Roast in a quick oven. Serve on toast, and pour around them a little good brown gravy. They should be sent to the table very hot.

For small birds, dress them nicely, split them down the back, cleaning out well, and drying on a napkin. Lay them

Fig. 36. 1. Red-Breasted Snipe; 2. Avoset; 3. Solitary Sandpiper; 4. Yellow-Shank Snipe; 5. Tell-Tale Snipe.

out flat on a hot gridiron over a clear fire. Turn frequently, and when done, sprinkle salt and pepper over them. Lay each bird on a slice of buttered toast. Spread butter over the birds, and set in the oven for a few minutes; serve while very hot.

Roast Partridge.

Let the birds hang as long as possible, then pluck and draw them; wipe but do not wash them, inside and out, and truss

50 THE KITCHEN.

them without the head, the same as for roast fowl. Put them into a hot oven, keep them well basted while cooking, and serve them on buttered toast, soaked in the dripping-pan, with a little butter poured over them, or with bread sauce and gravy

Fig. 37. 1. Esquimaux Curlew; 2. Red-Backed Snipe; 3. Willet, or Semi-Palmated Snipe; 4. Godwit Sandpiper.

Fig. 38. 1. Turn-Stone; 2. Ash-Colored Sandpiper; 3. Purre; 4. Black-Bellied Plover; 5. Red-Breasted Sandpiper.

GAME. 51

Woodcock.

Woodcocks should not be drawn, as their trails are considered a great delicacy. Pluck and wipe them well, truss them with the legs close to the body, skin the neck and head, and bring the beak round under the wing. Place a piece of toast in the dripping-pan under each bird to catch the trails. Baste frequently. Roast from 20 to 25 minutes. When done, serve the pieces of toast with the birds upon them. Pour a little gravy over them, and send some to the table in a tureen.

Fig. 39. 1. Rail; 2. Woodcock.

To Broil Quail or Woodcock.

After dressing, split down the back, sprinkle with salt and pepper, and lay them on a gridiron, the inside down; broil slowly at first; serve with cream gravy.

Roasted Quail.

These are cooked like woodcock, without drawing them, and are served on toast in the same manner.

Ragout of Wild Duck.

Ducks that have been dressed and left from the preceding day will answer for this purpose. Cut them into joints; reserve the legs, wings and breasts until wanted; put the trimmings into a stew-pan, with 2 onions and 1 pint of beef stock; let them simmer ¼ hour, and strain the gravy. Put an ounce of butter into a stew-pan; when melted, dredge in a little flour

Fig. 40. 1. Black, or Serf Duck; 2. Buffel-Headed Duck; 3. Female Duck; 4. Canada Goose; 5. Tufted Duck; 6. Golden-Eyed Duck; 7. Shoveler.

and pour in the gravy made from the bones, give it a boil, and strain again; add 1 glass Port wine, juice of ½ a lemon, and a pinch of cayenne; lay in the pieces of duck, and let the whole gradually warm through, but do not allow it to boil, as this will harden it. The gravy should not be too thick; a little orange juice improves it.

GAME. 53

Wild ducks are prepared for roasting the same as tame ones. To take away the fishy taste which wild fowl sometimes have, baste them for a few minutes with hot water, to which an onion and a little salt have been added. Then take away the pan, and baste with butter only.

Fig. 41. 1. Long-Tailed Duck; 2. Female; 3. Summer Duck; 4. Green-Winged Teal; 5. Canvas-Back Duck; 6. Red-Headed Duck; 7. Mallard.

Fried Rabbit.

Cut the rabbit into joints, and roll in flour ; have ready hot drippings or butter, and fry it a nice brown. Dredge a little flour into the pan, carefully add a little water to the gravy, and pour it around the pieces after they are laid on the platter.

Boiled Rabbit.

After it is skinned, let it lie fifteen minutes in water, to draw out the blood. Then put it into enough hot water to cover it, boil gently from $\frac{1}{2}$ to $\frac{3}{4}$ of an hour, according to its size and age. Dish it, and serve either with onion, mushroom or parsley and butter sauce.

OYSTERS.

Stewed Oysters.

Drain the liquor from the oysters, scald and strain it, to remove any pieces of shell and scum that may rise. To this liquor add to each quart of oysters, a pint each of milk and water, the amount of milk being a matter of taste. When scalded, season with salt, pepper, and a little nutmeg if the flavor is relished, ½ teacupful rolled cracker, and butter the size of an egg. Put in the oysters, and, when they begin to curl, which will be in 3 or 4 minutes, remove from the fire, and serve at once. If cooked too long, they become dark and tasteless.

Scalloped Oysters.

Butter a pudding dish, roll crackers very fine; put a layer of crackers, then a layer of oysters, season with salt and pepper, put small bits of butter over the oysters, fill the dish nearly full, having crackers on top; pour in sweet milk enough to soak the crackers; bake nearly an hour. If too dry when baking, add a little more milk and butter.

Oysters on the Shell.

Wash the shells, and put them on hot coals or upon the top of a hot stove, or bake them in a hot oven; open the shells with an oyster knife, taking care to lose none of the liquor, and serve quickly on hot plates, with toast. Oysters may be steamed in the shells, and are excellent, eaten in the same manner.

Fried Oysters.

Drain the oysters, and dry them by pressing between a soft cloth or napkin. Season with pepper and salt. Dip in well-

OYSTERS. 55

beaten egg, then in very fine cracker crumbs. If the oyster is not fully encrusted, repeat this process. Fry in plenty of hot lard, like doughnuts. Take up on unglazed paper to absorb the fat. Serve on a napkin, and garnish with parsley or coldslaw.

Broiled Oysters.

Select the large ones, used for frying, and first dip them in beaten egg, then in either cracker or bread crumbs, and cook upon a fine wire gridiron, over a quick fire. Toast should be made ready in advance, and a rich cream sauce poured over the whole. After pouring on the sauce, finely cut celery strewn over the top adds to their delicacy.

Roasted Oysters.

Take oysters in the shell, wash the shells clean, and lay them on hot coals ; when they are done they will begin to open. Remove the upper shell, and serve the oysters in the lower shell, with a little melted butter poured over each.

Oyster Fritters.

Chop a pint of oysters; make a batter of a pint of milk, a little salt and pepper, and flour enough to make a thin batter. Stir in the oysters. Fry in hot lard or butter. Drop them in from the spoon, and fry a delicate brown.

Oyster Pie.

Line a pudding-dish with puff paste, if not too rich. Cover with a plate the same size as the pudding dish, and on this place the upper crust. Put them into the oven to bake, and while they are there, make ready the filling, which is prepared as for stewed oysters, with a little more bread or cracker crumbs stirred in it. In 15 or 20 minutes the crusts should be done. Fill the oysters in the crust. Slip the baked upper crust on the top of the pie, and return it to the oven for 5 minutes. Serve at once.

Oyster Dressing.

For one chicken use 2 dozen or more oysters, chop very fine, season with ½ cup butter, pepper and salt to taste; mix with 2 cups of bread or cracker crumbs, and 1 quart milk. Cook in a saucepan. If not moist enough, add some of the oyster liquor.

Pickled Oysters.

To 100 oysters take 1 pint vinegar, and ½ ounce each of whole pepper and cloves, and a little mace. Scald the oysters in the liquor, drain them; boil the vinegar with the spices, and a part of the oyster liquor. Pour it over the oysters before they are quite cold. Let them stand a day or two before using.

Clams.

They may be roasted, stewed and fried the same as oysters. Care should be taken to have them as fresh as possible.

Clam Chowder.

The materials needed are clams, salt pork, onions, potatoes, sea-biscuit, plenty of seasoning and milk. First fry in the chowder kettle salt pork till nicely browned. In this fat, after removing the pork, fry the onions. Have the clams ready, and, when the onions are cooked, add water, and in alternate layers the sea biscuits, clam liquor and clams, potatoes, fried pork chopped fine, and the seasoning of pepper and salt, and sweet herbs if liked. Boil all together till the potatoes are nearly done, when remove from the kettle to a tureen, add a quart of milk and a little thickening to the gravy; when scalded pour it over the contents of the tureen. Serve at once.

CATSUPS.

Tomato Catsup.

Take 1 bushel fully ripe tomatoes; cut out any imperfect parts, and the green portions; put them in a porcelain kettle, adding just as little water as will keep them from burning. Peel and slice a half-dozen onions of medium size; boil until very soft. Strain through a sieve, return to the kettle, add 2 quarts good cider vinegar, 2 ounces each of ground allspice, black pepper and flour mustard, 1 ounce ground cloves, ¼ ounce cayenne pepper, 2 pounds sugar. Mix all together well with 1½ teacupfuls salt; return to the kettle and boil 2 hours; stir frequently to prevent scorching. Bottle and seal.

Cold Catsup.

Skin ½ a peck of tomatoes without scalding, chop fine, and drain in a colander. Cut 2 roots of horse-radish in small slips, and chop 2 stalks of celery and 3 red peppers. Mix all together with a quart of vinegar, a cup of nasturtiums, ½ a cup each of salt and sugar, a tablespoonful each of ground cinnamon and cloves, 1 teaspoonful each of mace and black pepper, and a cup of mixed black and white mustard.

Walnut or Butternut Catsup.

Gather the nuts while still soft, so that they can be pierced with a pin. Pound them to a pulp, and let them lie a fortnight in salt water; then drain them, and pour a pint of boiling vinegar over the nuts, and strain it out. To each quart of this liquor add 3 tablespoonfuls of pepper, 1 of ginger, 2 of cloves and 1 of nutmeg. Boil an hour after mixing the spices well.

SALADS.

Salad Dressing.

Materials: 1 cup milk, 1 of vinegar, 3 eggs, 1 tablespoonful each of sugar and olive oil or butter, ¼ tablespoonful of salt and a scant tablespoonful of mustard. Stir the oil, sugar, salt and mustard in a bowl together until perfectly smooth; then add the well-beaten eggs, stir all thoroughly, and add the vinegar, and lastly milk. Put in a farina kettle, and let it boil together until it thickens like custard.

Lobster Salad.

Boil the lobster ½ an hour; remove the shell, being careful to take out the vein in the back. Chop the meat, or pick it fine. Arrange the lobster in the plate, as in Fig. 42. Make a good salad of celery, lettuce or endive, chopped red beets and

Fig. 42.

hard-boiled eggs. For dressing take 3 or 4 tablespoonfuls of oil, 2 of vinegar, 1 teaspoonful of made mustard, and the yolks of two hard-boiled eggs. Sometimes a very small quantity of anchovy sauce is added. Mix these ingredients well with the meat from the body of the lobster. Arrange it

SALADS.   59

around the lobster, garnish with sliced beets, cucumbers, the yolks and whites of eggs, using taste in blending the colors.

Celery Salad.

One head of cabbage, 3 bunches of celery, chopped very fine. Take 1 teacupful of vinegar, lump of butter size of an egg, yolks of 2 eggs, 1 teaspoonful mustard, 1 of salt, pinch of cayenne pepper, 2 teaspoonfuls of sugar. Mix these well; put the mixture on the stove, and heat until it thickens, stirring all the time; when cold, add two tablespoonfuls of rich, sweet cream. If not moist enough, add cold vinegar.

Potato Salad.

Boil the potatoes tender, and when cold cut them into little cubes, or slices. Lay loosely on the plate from which they are to be served. Chop a little onion very fine, and strew over the potato. Pour over it a nice salad dressing.

Chicken Salad.

Chop the white parts of 3 chickens, or pick them to pieces, as preferred; add twice the bulk of celery either chopped or cut small. Make a dressing of the yolks of 3 uncooked eggs, 1 tablespoonful mustard, 3 tablespoonfuls sugar, 1 teaspoonful salt, a pinch of cayenne pepper, $\frac{1}{3}$ cupful vinegar, $\frac{1}{4}$ pint of olive oil and $\frac{1}{2}$ a lemon. Beat the yolks well and add mustard, sugar, etc., until smooth; then, by degrees, add the oil, vinegar and lemon juice. The dressing should be quite thick after the last oil is added. Put it on ice until wanted.

Oyster Sauce (to serve with Fish, Boiled Poultry, etc.).

Open 3 dozen oysters carefully and save their liquor. Strain it into a clean saucepan, put in the oysters, and let them just come to the boiling point. Take them out at once, strain the liquor again, and put enough butter with it mixed with milk to make 1 pint altogether. When this is ready and very smooth, put in the oysters, which should be bearded to be really nice. Keep it hot till wanted, but *do not let it boil,* or the oysters will immediately harden. Some may like a seasoning of cayenne or anchovy sauce.

Butter-Maitre d'Hotel—Cold Sauce.

Mix thoroughly with a wooden spoon ¼ pound of butter, 2 dessert-spoonfuls of minced parsley, salt and pepper to taste, and the juice of one large lemon. This may be put under or over the fish it is to be served with. With 4 tablespoonfuls white or Béchamel sauce, 2 ounces white stock and 2 ounces of the above, simmered 1 minute together, a hot sauce is made.

Celery Sauce for Boiled Turkey, Poultry, etc.

Boil 6 heads of celery in salt and water until tender, and cut it into pieces 2 inches long, Put 1 pint of white stock into a stew-pan, 2 blades of mace and 1 small bunch of savory herbs, and let it simmer ½ hour to extract their flavor. Then strain the liquor, add the celery and a thickening of butter and arrowroot; just before serving add ½ pint of cream, boil it up, and squeeze in a little lemon juice. If necessary, add a seasoning of salt and white pepper. This may be made brown by using gravy instead of white stock, and flavoring it with mushroom catsup or Worcestershire sauce.

Cream Sauce for Fish or White Dishes.

Put 2 ounces of butter into a saucepan, dredge into it 1 teaspoonful of flour, and keep shaking around till the butter is melted; add ⅛ pint of cream, salt and cayenne to taste, and stir till it boils. Let it just simmer for 5 minutes, when add either pounded mace or lemon juice to taste, to give it a flavor.

YEAST AND BREAD.

Potato Yeast.

Take 2 quarts of water to 1 ounce of hops. Boil them 15 minutes; add 1 quart of cold water, and let it boil for a few minutes; strain, and add ½ pound of flour, putting the latter into a basin, and pouring the water on slowly to prevent its getting lumpy; ¼ pound of brown sugar, a handful of fine salt. Let it stand 3 days, stirring it occasionally. When it ferments well, add 6 potatoes, which have been boiled, mashed and run through a colander, making them as smooth as possible. This yeast will keep a long while, and has the advantage of not requiring any yeast to start it with. It rises so quickly that a less quantity of it must be put in than of ordinary yeast.

Dried Yeast.

Peel 6 good-sized potatoes, and boil until tender. Have ready in a stone crock 3 pints of flour; while the potatoes are hot work them through a colander into the dry flour. Boil a large handful of hops 15 minutes in 3 pints of water; strain out the hops, add the water to the flour and potatoes, mix well, and when almost cold, add enough cold water to make it as thin as bread sponge. Have half a pint of dry yeast soaked soft, and stir it in. Let the yeast rise, stirring it down several times, then add to it 3 quarts of sifted corn meal, mix thoroughly, roll, cut into cakes, and dry quickly.

Bread.

Add 1 quart of water to ½ teacupful potato yeast, and as much flour as can be mixed in it with a spoon. Let it stand over night. In the morning add 1 pint milk, with enough flour to make a soft dough. Let it remain until it is quite light, then knead thoroughly again, and make into loaves. Let it rise again; bake in a steady but not too hot oven.

Brown Bread.

Three cups of corn-meal, 2 cups of rye flour, 3 cups of sour milk, 1 cup of N. O. molasses, 1 cup of raisins, 2 even teaspoonfuls salt, 3 even teaspoonfuls soda. Sift the meal and flour together; mix the molasses, sour milk, salt and soda—the soda dissolved in a little warm water—and, while the mixture is effervescing, pour it into the flour, beating with a wooden spoon until smooth. Grease a pudding boiler, and pour in the batter, a little at a time—adding the raisins in layers—until the mould is filled to within about two inches of the top. Cover closely, place in a kettle of boiling water, and cook 4 or 5 hours.

Breakfast Corn Bread.

Two eggs, ½ cupful each of sweet milk and sour, ½ teaspoonful each of salt and saleratus; corn-meal enough to make a thin batter. Beat the eggs very light, add the salt and sweet milk; stir saleratus into the sour milk, and add it to the rest; put in the corn-meal a little at a time. The batter should be quite as thin as for batter cakes. Beat it hard for a few minutes, then pour into a well-buttered tin, and bake in a quick oven. When done, remove from the pan, cut in squares, and serve.

Milk Sponge Bread.

Put into a pitcher or jar a pint of boiling water, a teaspoonful of sugar, ¼ teaspoonful each of soda and salt. When cool enough to bear your hand in it, add flour to make a thick batter. Beat it well, and put the vessel in water as hot as can be used without scalding the mixture. Keep up a uniform temperature till the "rising" or "emptyings" are light. If set

Yeast and Bread. 63

in the morning early, they will doubtless be ready before noon to make a sponge. Add a quart of warm milk, and the flour as for other bread. When this sponge is very light, make into loaves, and let them rise again, but care should be taken not to let them rise too long, or the bread will be dry and tasteless.

Rye Bread.

Put 2 quarts of rye flour into a stone jar; stir into it 1 cup of yeast, 2 teaspoonfuls of salt, and enough water to moisten well. Let it rise over night in a warm place. In the morning stir it down well; do not add more flour, but put into well-buttered pans; as soon as light, bake in a slow oven.

Graham Bread.

To 1 pint of the bread sponge take 1 pint of milk (water will do), add a little salt, soda and sugar. Stir in sufficient graham flour to make batter just stiff enough to drop from the spoon. Fill a pint can a little over half full, let it rise until three-fourths full, then place in a kettle of boiling water and let it steam about an hour, according to size of can, etc.

Excellent Corn Bread.

To 3 cups corn-meal—the yellow is preferable—take 3½ cups wheat flour, 1 cup molasses, 1 quart thick milk, 1 teaspoonful soda, and 2 teaspoonfuls of salt. Mix quickly, pour into a basin, and steam 2 hours; then bake ½ to ¾ of an hour.

Rusk.

Take 4 cups bread dough, 1 cup sugar, ½ cup butter, 3 eggs. Work these well into the dough, adding flour as needed; let it rise; mould into biscuits, and let them rise again. Currants and spices may be added if desired. Brush the top with a little sweetened milk, and bake to a delicate brown.

BREAKFAST ROLLS, ETC.

Tea Rolls.

Two quarts of flour, 1 quart of sweet milk, ¼ of a cup of butter, and a cake of compressed yeast. Make a soft batter at night, if the rolls are desired hot for breakfast, using only half of the flour. The butter can either be rubbed into the flour, or dissolved in the tepid milk. Early in the morning add the other half of the flour, and let the sponge rise again. Then make into long, narrow rolls for baking, or roll and cut with a large biscuit cutter, and tuck up like French breakfast rolls. Let them rise for a few minutes, and bake in a quick oven.

French Rolls.

One pint of milk, 1 small cup of home-made yeast (you can try the baker's), flour enough to make a stiff batter, raise over night; in the morning add 1 egg, 1 tablespoonful of butter, and flour enough to make it stiff to roll. Mix it well, and let it rise; then knead it again (to make it fine and white), roll out, cut with a round tin, and fold over; put them in a pan and cover very close. Set them in a warm place until they are very light, bake quickly, and you will have delicious rolls.

Maryland Biscuit.

Rub into 2 quarts of flour 1 small teacupful lard and the usual quantity of salt. Mix it up with just enough water to make a stiff dough, and beat from half an hour to an hour. It should be worked until the blisters are constantly snapping and the dough is waxy. After the dough is once mixed, there should be no more flour worked in. When it is all right, if you break off a piece quickly it snaps off short, and, in cutting a piece off

BREAKFAST ROLLS, ETC.

with a sharp knife, the holes or pores where you have cut it are small, and of an even size. Now break off the dough in small pieces, and work each piece into a nice biscuit shape, and press it with the lower part of the thumb, where it joins the hand, to make the indentation; prick, and bake quickly in a hot oven. The biscuit should be a light brown in the centre of the top and on the bottom, but not all over, and not hard.

Vienna Rolls.

One quart flour, $\frac{1}{2}$ teaspoonful salt, 2 teaspoonfuls baking powder, 1 tablespoonful lard, 1 pint milk. Sift together flour, salt and baking powder; rub in the lard cold; add the milk, and mix into a smooth dough in the bowl, easy to be handled. Flour the board, then roll to the thickness of $\frac{1}{2}$ an inch, cut it out with a large round cutter, fold one half over on the other by doubling it, lay them on a greased baking sheet without touching, wash them over with a little milk, to glaze them, and bake in a hot oven 15 minutes.

Rye Breakfast Cakes.

Take 2 cupfuls of rye-meal, 1 cupful of flour, 2 well-beaten eggs, whites and yolks beaten separately, 1 pint of sweet milk, $\frac{1}{2}$ tablespoonful of salt. Stir together, adding the whites of the eggs last. Butter heavy ironstone china teacups, fill each half full of batter, set them in a pan, bake for 30 minutes.

Buckwheat Cakes.

Take 1 pint each of milk and water, $\frac{1}{2}$ cake of compressed yeast, or 1 cup of potato or hop yeast, and sufficient buckwheat flour to make a smooth batter. Let it rise, and, just before baking, add a couple of tablespoonfuls of molasses or sugar, to brown them. Many use water alone instead of half milk.

Graham Biscuits.

Take 3 cups graham flour, 1 cup wheat flour; rub into it 2 tablespoonfuls butter, ½ cup sugar, a beaten egg. Add 2 teaspoonfuls baking powder, a little salt, and enough milk to make a soft dough. Roll thin, cut out, and bake quickly.

Raised Muffins.

Make a batter at night with 1 quart of sweet milk, ¾ teacupful of yeast, 2 tablespoonfuls of sugar, and 2 of butter or lard, 1 teaspoonful of salt, with enough flour to make it moderately thick, but so that it will pour well. Let it stand in a warm, not hot, place over night. In the morning, stir in 2 well-beaten eggs, and bake in muffin-rings in a quick oven.

Muffins without Yeast.

Take 1 pint of sweet milk, 2 eggs, 1 large tablespoonful of butter, 3 teaspoonfuls of baking powder, well mixed and sifted with the flour, 1 teaspoonful of salt, and flour to make the batter stiff enough to drop from the spoon into the muffin-rings.

Graham Muffins.

One egg, 1 tablespoonful of sugar, 1 quart of graham flour, 2 teaspoonfuls of baking powder, ½ teaspoonful of salt, 2 tablespoonfuls of butter, and milk enough to make a soft batter.

Waffles.

A quart of sweet milk, 2 tablespoonfuls of butter, 3 beaten eggs, 3 teaspoonfuls of baking powder, a teaspoonful of salt, and as much sugar as is liked by the eaters. With the iron heated up while beating the eggs and mixing, one can have the waffles on the table in five or six minutes from beginning to prepare them. Only skill enough is needed to cook them quickly, yet just enough, without scorching.

Breakfast Rolls, etc.

Raised Waffles.

One quart of milk slightly warmed, 5 cups of flour, 3 eggs well beaten, ⅔ of a cup of home-made yeast, or half a penny's worth of baker's, and ½ a teaspoonful of salt. Set as sponge over night. In the morning add 2 tablespoonfuls of melted butter. Have the waffle-irons very hot and well greased.

Strawberry Shortcake.

Into 1 cupful of sour cream stir ½ teaspoonful of soda, add 1 tablespoonful of melted butter, and flour enough to make a stiff dough. Roll it out to fit in a large pie-pan, and bake in a quick oven. Split open, butter well, and spread a pint of sugared berries between the layers, and as many more over the top.

Make the dough as for soda biscuits; bake in deep jelly-pans or pie-tins; split the cakes, and spread with the sugared berries. Raspberries, peaches, etc., are nice to use in the same way.

Cream Fritters.

One pint sweet cream, 1 pint milk, 1½ pints flour, into which mix 3 teaspoonfuls baking powder, 1 teaspoonful salt, 4 eggs, the yolks and whites beaten separately. Fry in hot fat, like doughnuts, except that these are dropped in from the spoon.

Hominy Fritters.

Two cups cold boiled hominy, 2 eggs, 1 cup milk, 1 cup flour, a pinch of salt, ½ teaspoonful baking powder. Drop from a spoon into hot lard, and fry brown.

Sally Lunn.

Three pints sifted flour, 1 pint milk, 3 eggs, ½ cup butter, 1 cup sugar, 1 gill yeast, or 2 teaspoonfuls baking powder, 1 teaspoonful salt. If yeast is used, it will require 3 or 4 hours to rise. Bake in a loaf.

PUDDINGS.

To insure success, all the ingredients should be good—the milk and eggs fresh, and the fruits of excellent quality.

Cold Apple Pudding.

Peel and core 10 or 12 good baking apples, slice them, and put ¼ pound of sugar, an ounce of butter, a sprinkling of nutmeg and grated lemon peel, into a saucepan with them, and

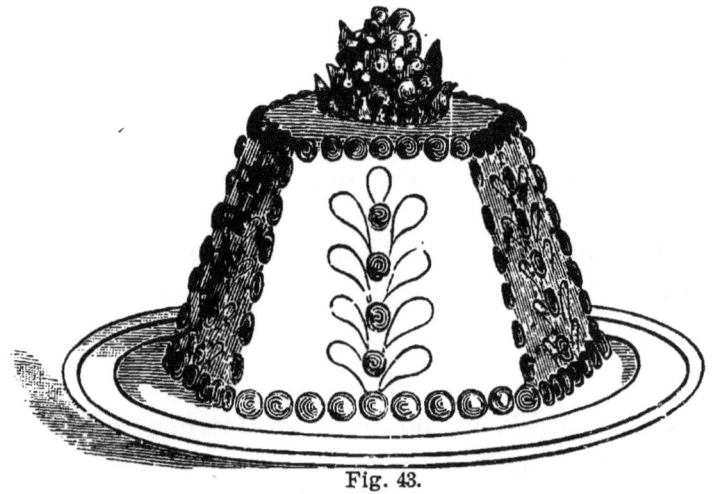

Fig. 43.

cook until soft; set it by to cool. Line a mould with good pudding paste, fill in the apples, cover with paste, tie in a cloth, and boil 1¼ hours. Turn it out, and ornament with a flower on the top, as seen in Fig. 43.

Apple Sago Pudding.

Peel ½ a dozen sour apples, and, if perfect, simply remove the cores; if not, cut in halves and place together again. Put the apples in a buttered pudding dish, and sprinkle sugar over

PUDDINGS. 69

them. Cover the dish with a plate, set in the oven, and bake until the apples are well done. While they are baking, boil 1 cup of sago in 2 cups of water, adding a little salt. When the sago turns to a transparent jelly, it is done. Remove from the stove, stir in 2 to 4 tablespoonfuls of sugar, according to the sourness of the apples, and pour the sago into the pudding dish over the apples. Return to the oven, and let it remain there until it is browned on top.

Apple Pudding.

Pare and core 8 or 9 juicy apples. Put them into a pudding dish, half filled with water; cover closely, and bake until tender. Drain off the water, fill each apple with jelly, and season with any spice preferred. Let them stand until cool. Scald 1 pint of milk, into which stir ½ pound of macaroons, pounded fine, a little salt, a tablespoonful of corn starch, 3 tablespoonfuls of sugar. Boil all together 1 or 2 minutes, and when cool add the whites of 3 eggs, beaten to a stiff froth. Pour over the apples, and bake 20 or 30 minutes. Eat with cream.

Tapioca and Fruit Pudding.

To 3 pints of cold water add 1 teacupful of tapioca; put on the back of the stove, where it will be warm, but not get hot, and let it remain until soft. It will take from 1½ to 2 hours. Have ready, peeled and sliced, 12 good-sized sour apples, and add them to the tapioca, with a heaping teacupful of sugar. Bake until the apples are thoroughly cooked, and the tapioca becomes like jelly. It is nicer when allowed to cool before serving, and should be eaten with cream and sugar.

Peach Batter Pudding.

For a quart of peeled and stoned peaches, cut in halves, take 1 tablespoonful of butter, 1 teaspoonful baking powder, 1 quart sweet milk, 3 eggs, 2 cups of flour, and ½ teaspoonful of salt. Lay the peaches in a well-buttered earthen baking dish. Sift the flour; stir into it (dry) the salt and baking powder, then rub in the butter until perfectly fine. Beat the eggs, and add them and the milk together, pouring in slowly, and stirring all the time, until the batter is smooth, then pour it over the peaches. Bake about ½ an hour. Serve warm with butter and sugar, or with sweetened cream.

Sunderland Pudding.

Take 6 eggs, 4 tablespoonfuls flour, 1 pint sweet milk, and a little salt. Beat the yolks well, and mix smoothly with the flour; then add the milk and the whites beaten to a stiff froth. Bake in a quick oven.

Rice Pudding.

To 1 cupful of boiled rice add 4 eggs, 1 cupful each of sugar and raisins, a little nutmeg, and 1½ pints of milk. Bake until the milk is like custard, and brown on top.

Amber Pudding.

Mix together ¼ pound of sugar and the same each of butter and bread crumbs. Add 3 eggs, well beaten, and 3 tablespoonfuls orange marmalade. Mix the butter and sugar together, then the eggs and bread crumbs, and lastly the marmalade. Put the whole in a mould, cover closely, and steam 2 hours.

Steamed Suet Pudding.

Two cups sweet milk, 1 cup molasses, 3 cups flour, one cup each of raisins, currants and suet, one teaspoonful soda. Put in a 2-quart basin, and steam 2 hours.

Delmonico Pudding.

A quart of milk, 3 tablespoonfuls corn starch. Mix the starch with cold water, and stir into the boiling milk. Mix 6

PUDDINGS. 71

tablespoonfuls of white sugar with the yolks of 5 eggs, and pour into the starch. Put into a pudding dish, and bake. Beat the whites of 5 eggs with 6 tablespoonfuls of sugar, and flavor with vanilla ; drop with a spoon on the pudding, and brown slightly in the oven.

Snow Pudding.

One-half package of Coxe's gelatine, pour over it a cup of cold water, and add 1½ cups of sugar ; when soft, add 1 cup of boiling water, juice of 1 lemon, and the whites of 4 well-beaten eggs ; beat all together until very light. Put in a glass dish, and pour over it custard made as follows : 1 pint milk, yolks of 4 eggs, and grated rind of 1 lemon ; boil. Splendid.

Baked Indian Pudding.

Scald 1 quart of milk. Stir into a little cold milk 1 teacupful Indian meal (the yellow is preferable), and add to the boiling milk, stirring until it thickens, but no longer, or it will not bake well. When nearly cold, add 2 well-beaten eggs, a pinch of salt, a pint of cold milk ; sweeten with half sugar and half molasses, and flavor with nutmeg. Bake about 1 hour, or until water bubbles from the top. It is best served hot.

Frosted Lemon Pudding.

Take a pint of bread or cake crumbs, 1 quart of milk, the juice and grated peel of a lemon, the yolks of 3 eggs, and sweeten to the taste. When baked, cover over with jelly, make a frosting of the whites of the eggs and sugar, pour over the top, and set in the oven a few minutes to brown.

The Queen of Puddings.

One and one-half cup white sugar ; 2 cups fine dry bread crumbs ; 5 eggs ; 1 tablespoonful of butter ; vanilla, rose-water or lemon seasoning ; 1 quart fresh, rich milk, and ½ a cup jelly or jam. Rub the butter into a cup of sugar ; beat the yolks very light, and stir these together to a cream. The bread crumbs soaked in milk come next, then the seasoning. Bake in a buttered pudding-dish—a large one, and but two-thirds full—until the custard is "set." Draw to the mouth of the oven, spread over with jam or other nice fruit conserve. Cover this with a meringue made of the whipped whites and ½ a cup of sugar. Shut the oven, and bake until the meringue begins to color. Eat cold, with cream. In strawberry season, substitute fresh fruit for preserves. It is then delicious.

Chocolate Pudding.

Pour 1 pint of boiling milk over 4 ounces of grated chocolate; dissolve 3 tablespoonfuls of corn starch in 1 pint of milk, add 3 beaten eggs, 3 tablespoonfuls of sugar, 1 teaspoonful of vanilla extract. Mix, and pour into the milk and chocolate. Let it boil 1 minute, stirring briskly; pour out into cups or moulds, and set away in a cold place until wanted.

John Bull's Own Plum Pudding.

One-half pound bread crumbs, ¼ pound flour, 1 pound each of currants, seedless raisins, moist sugar, mixed candied peel, 1 teaspoonful salt, 1 of mixed spices, 8 eggs, ¼ pint brandy. Mix all thoroughly, after chopping the suet, and seeding, stemming and washing the fruit. Add the eggs, and lastly the brandy, after beating for 25 minutes; butter a mould and fill it; scald a clean cloth and flour it; put the pudding in, tie it down, and boil 13 hours.

Baked Plum Pudding.

Two pounds of flour, 1 pound each of raisins, currants and suet, 2 eggs, 1 pint milk, a few slices of candied peel. Chop the suet finely, mix with it the flour, currants, raisins, ½ nutmeg and candied peel. Moisten with the well-beaten eggs, and add sufficient milk to make the pudding of the

PUDDINGS. 73

consistency of any thick batter. Put it in a buttered dish, and bake in a good oven from 2¼ to 2½ hours. Half the quantity is enough for an ordinary-sized family.

A Simple Bread Pudding.

Pour 1 quart boiling milk into a dish filled with bread crumbs. Stir in 2 beaten eggs and dust the top over with cinnamon. Bake 20 minutes. Serve with sugar and cream.

Aunt Helen's Country Pudding.

Place a layer of stale bread rolled fine, in the bottom of a pudding dish, then a layer of any kind of fruit; sprinkle on a little sugar, then another layer of bread crumbs and of fruit; and so on until the dish is full, the top layer being crumbs. Make a custard as for pies, add a pint of milk, and mix. Pour it over the top of the pudding, and bake until the fruit is cooked.

Apple Dumplings.

Pare and core medium-sized juicy, tart apples. Make a dough as for soda biscuit, and fold around each apple. Place in a steamer over a kettle of boiling water. Steam till the apples are soft. Eat with sweetened cream, or butter and sugar creamed and flavored with nutmeg. They may be baked instead of steamed.

Rice Pudding without Eggs.

Two quarts of milk, ½ teacupful of rice, a little less than a teacupful of sugar, the same quantity of raisins, a teaspoonful of cinnamon or allspice; wash the rice and put it with the rest of the ingredients into the milk. Bake rather slowly from 2 to 3 hours; stir two or three times the first hour of baking. If properly done, this pudding is delicious.

SAUCES.

Pudding Sauce.

Rub 1 cup sugar and ½ cup butter to a cream; add the beaten white of an egg, ½ teaspoonful extract of lemon or rose, and 1 cup boiling water, in which has been stirred 1 teaspoonful corn starch.

Wine Sauce.

The yolks of 4 eggs, 1 teaspoonful flour, 2 tablespoonfuls each of butter and sugar, a pinch of salt, ½ pint of sherry or Madeira. Put the butter and flour into a saucepan, and stir over the fire until it thickens, then mix the other ingredients, adding the wine last. Separate the yolks from the whites of the 4 eggs, beat up the former, and stir them briskly to the sauce. Let it remain over the fire until it is on the point of simmering, but do not let it boil, or it will curdle. This makes a delicious sauce for plum, suet and bread puddings.

Lemon Sauce.

The rind and juice of 1 lemon, 1 tablespoonful each of flour and butter, 1 large wineglassful each of sherry and water, sugar to taste, the yolks of 4 eggs. Prepared like the above, except that the rind of the lemon is rubbed on the sugar, and the juice is strained into the sauce.

Strawberry Sauce.

Rub 1 cup of sugar and ½ cup butter to a cream; add the beaten white of an egg and 1 cup crushed strawberries.

Raspberry Sauce.

This sauce is made the same as the above, raspberries being used instead of strawberries.

DISHES FOR DESSERT.

Spanish Cream.

Put half a box of gelatine in a quart of sweet milk, and let it scald until the gelatine is entirely melted; then add the yolks of 4 eggs, previously well beaten with a cup of sugar; when scalding, but not boiling, stir in the whites of the eggs after beating to a stiff froth. Season as desired. Strain into moulds.

Apples and Rice.

Peel and core as many nice apples as are needed to arrange in a dish like Fig. 44. Boil them soft in a light syrup. Cook ¼ pound of rice in milk, with a spoonful of sugar and a pinch

Fig. 44.

of salt. Put some of the rice in the bottom of the dish, arrange the apples in a pyramid with the rice between, and ornament with real or artificial leaves.

Orange Charlotte.

For 2 moulds of medium size soak ¼ box gelatine in ½ cup of water for 2 hours. Add 1½ cups boiling water, and strain. Then add 2 cups sugar, 1 cup of orange juice and pulp, and the juice of 1 lemon. Stir until the mixture begins to cool, or about 5 minutes; then add the whites of 6 eggs, beaten to a stiff froth. Beat the whole until so stiff that it will only just pour into moulds lined with sections of orange. Set away to cool.

Whipped Cream.

To every pint of cream allow 3 ounces of pounded sugar, 1 glass of sherry or any kind of sweet wine, the rind of ½ a lemon, the white of 1 egg. Rub the sugar on the lemon rind, and pound it till quite fine ; beat up the white of the egg to a stiff froth ; put the cream into a large bowl with the sugar, wine and beaten egg, and whip it to a froth. As fast as the froth rises, take it off with a skimmer and put it on a sieve to drain, in a cool place. The cream will be firmer if made the day before it is wanted. It should be whipped in a cool place, and in summer over ice, if it is obtainable.

Omelette Soufflée.

Four eggs ; beat the whites and yolks separately. To the yolks add 3 tablespoonfuls powdered sugar and 1 teaspoonful extract of vanilla. Stir the eggs and sugar into the whites very gently. Drop by the spoonful into buttered pans, and bake in a moderate oven. They should be eaten as soon as done, or they will fall.

Charlotte Russe.

Take 18 ladies' fingers, as they are sometimes called; brush the edges of them with the white of an egg, and line the bottom of a plain round mould, placing them like a star or rosette. Stand them upright around the edge, placing them so closely that the white of the egg may connect them firmly, and place this case in the oven for about 5 minutes to dry the egg. Whisk ¾ of a pint of cream to a stiff froth, add to it 1 tablespoonful powdered sugar, ½ ounce melted isinglass or gelatine,

¼ teaspoonful vanilla. Fill the mould with it, and cover the top with a slice of sponge cake cut in the shape of the mould. Place it on ice, and let it remain until ready for the table; then turn it on a dish, remove the mould, and serve.

Iced Oranges.

Peel a few oranges carefully, and pull them apart into thin portions. Whip the white of an egg with a wineglassful of water, and add a dessert spoonful of powdered sugar. Mix

Fig. 45.

all thoroughly together, and strain through a sieve into a flat vessel. Dip the fruit, with the white pith removed, into this mixture, roll carefully into sifted white sugar, and then place in rows to dry. Arrange as shown in Fig. 45.

A Good Dessert.

Of raspberries may be made of 1 large teacupful of cracker crumbs, 1 quart milk, the yolks of 3 eggs, 1 whole egg, and ½ cup of sugar. Flavor with vanilla, adding a little pinch of salt. Bake in a moderate oven. When done, spread over the top, while hot, a pint of well-sugared raspberries. Then beat the whites of the 3 eggs very stiff, with 2 tablespoonfuls sugar, a little lemon extract, or whatever one prefers. Spread this over the berries, and bake a light brown.

PIES, TARTS, ETC.

In making pastry, always sift the flour. Rub the butter or lard into it before adding the water, which should be as cold as possible. If lard is used, add salt; stir quickly. Many prefer cutting it with a knife instead of rubbing it in with the hands.

A Plain Pie Crust.

For two pies, 1 cup of lard, or lard and butter together, ¼ cup water, 3 cups flour, 1 teaspoonful salt.

Apple Pie.

Fill the pie crust with some juicy apples, pared and sliced thin. To each pie take 1 small cup sugar; butter, the size of a walnut, 1 teaspoonful flour, ⅛ of a grated nutmeg; rub well together, strew the seasoning over the apples, and add 2 or 3 tablespoonfuls water, according to the juiciness of the apples. Pinch the edges of the upper crust close, and bake at once.

Lemon Cream Pie.

One teacup powdered sugar, 1 tablespoonful butter, 1 egg, juice and grated rind of 1 lemon, 1 teacup boiling water, 1 tablespoonful corn starch dissolved in cold water; stir the corn starch into the hot water; add the butter and sugar, and when cold, the lemon and egg. Bake in open tart.

Lemon Pie.

Six eggs (less 2 whites), 2 cups of white sugar, a little salt, 1 cup of sweet milk, 2 tablespoonfuls of corn starch dissolved in the milk, 2 large lemons, juice and rind; bake slowly until set. Meringue for the top; whites of 2 eggs beaten with 6 tablespoonfuls of powdered sugar; bake to a light brown.

Pies, Tarts, etc.

Squash Pie.

To 1 quart of boiled milk, take 1 pint of strained squash, 2 cups sugar, 4 eggs, 1 teaspoonful salt, a few drops lemon extract or vanilla, ½ teaspoonful each of ginger, cinnamon and nutmeg. Bake with one crust in rather deep plates.

Pumpkin Pie.

Stew the pumpkin with just enough water to prevent burning. When soft, rub through a colander, and to each large teacupful add 1 pint milk or cream, 2 eggs, 1 cup sugar and flavoring to taste.

Apple Custard Pie.

Stew sour apples, rub them through a colander, add 3 well-beaten eggs, 1 cup each of butter and flour. Flavor with nutmeg. The above amount of seasoning will make 3 pies, and for each, 1 cup of sauce is needed.

Peach Custard Pie.

Use 1 crust; peel peaches and halve them, and turn the hollow side upward; sweeten as you would a peach pie; take 1 egg, a pinch of salt, 1 tablespoonful of sugar; beat; add milk enough to cover the peaches; bake. Eat when partly cool.

Potato Pie.

For 2 pies, boil 1 quart of sweet milk, and then stir into it 1 cup of grated potato. When cool, add 3 well-beaten eggs; sugar and nutmeg to taste. Bake with one crust. Eat the day it is baked.

Orange Pie.

Take 4 good-sized oranges, peel, seed, and cut in thin, small pieces. Strew 1 cup sugar over them, and let them stand. Into 1 quart of nearly boiling milk stir 1½ tablespoonfuls corn starch, and the yolks of 3 eggs. When this is done, mix the oranges with it, and put it in a lower crust already baked. Make a meringue of the whites of the eggs and ½ cup sugar, spread it on the top, and brown in the oven.

Cocoanut Pie.

One cupful grated cocoanut, 1 cup sugar, 1 quart milk, 1 tablespoonful butter, 3 eggs. Flavor with nutmeg. Bake in a deep pie-plate.

Mince Pie.

To 3 lbs. finely chopped beef add 6 lbs. apples, 1 lb. suet, 2 lbs. raisins, 2 lbs. currants, 1 lb. citron, 2 ozs. candied lemon, 1 oz. mace, 1 oz. cinnamon, 1 oz. nutmeg, 1 lb. sugar, 1 pint molasses or syrup, and 1 quart cider. Seed the raisins, and chop half of them ; chop the apples, thoroughly wash the currants, and slice the citron very thin. Mix well, put over the fire, cook slowly till the apples are done. If not sweet as liked, add more sugar ; if too stiff, increase the amount of cider.

Medium Puff Paste.

To every pound of flour take 8 ounces butter, 4 ounces lard, and not quite ½ pint water. Mix the flour to a smooth paste with the water, then roll it out 3 times ; the first time, covering the paste with butter ; the second, with lard ; and the third, with butter ; and it will be ready for use.

French Puff Paste.

Take equal quantities of flour and butter, say 1 pound of each, ½ saltspoonful of salt, the yolks of 2 eggs, rather more than ¼ pint of water. Sift the flour. Press all the water from the butter. Put the flour on the pasteboard, work lightly into it 2 ounces of the butter; then make a hole in the centre, and into it put the yolks of 2 eggs, the salt, and about ¼ pint of water; knead quickly, and, when smooth, roll it out into a square ¼ inch thick. Put the butter in a ball on the paste, and

Pies, Tarts, etc.

fold the paste securely over it. Roll it lightly with the rolling-pin, but not thin enough to allow the butter to break through. Keep the board well dredged. This rolling gives it the first turn; now fold the paste in three and roll it again. If the weather is warm, cool it between each rolling. Continue this process until it has had six turnings in all. If properly made and baked, this crust should rise in the oven 5 or 6 inches. The butter must be kept cool, or the paste will not answer at all.

Helen's Tart Shells.

Take ⅔ of a cupful of lard, 1 tablespoonful of white sugar, 5 tablespoonfuls cold water, and the white of an egg well beaten. Mould like pie-crust, cut with tart-shell cutter, and bake.

Apple Tarts.

Cook soft 10 or 12 tart apples, rub them through a colander, add 3 well-beaten eggs, grated juice and rind of 1 or 2 lemons, butter the size of an egg, 1½ cups sugar. Mix well. Line tart pans with puff paste, and fill with the sauce. Bake quickly.

German Puffs.

Take ½ pint of new milk, 2 ounces of flour, 2 eggs, 2 ounces melted butter, a little salt and butter. Beat the eggs well, then mix all the ingredients together, and put into little cups half full for baking. Bake 15 minutes in a hot oven.

Ginger Cream.

Slice finely 3 ounces preserved ginger, put it into a basin with 2 dessert spoonfuls of syrup, the well-beaten yolks of 4 eggs, and 1 pint cream. Mix these ingredients well together, and stir them over the fire for about 10 minutes, or until the mixture thickens; then take it off the fire, whisk till nearly cold, sweeten to taste, add 1 ounce gelatine, which should be melted and strained, and serve the cream in a glass dish.

CAKES.

In these, as in bread and pastry, good flour is requisite as well as good butter. Indeed, all the materials should be first-class. Always sift the baking powder with the flour, and rub the butter and sugar to a cream, adding the well-beaten yolks of the eggs to them, then the milk and flour by degrees, and lastly the whites beaten to a stiff froth. After these are added it should be beaten as little as possible.

Cookies.

One cup sugar, ⅔ cup butter, 4 cups flour, ½ cup sour milk, and a teaspoonful each of soda, baking powder and caraway seed.

One cup sugar, ½ cup butter, 2 eggs, 3 tablespoonfuls sweet milk and 1 heaping teaspoonful baking powder. Flavor with nutmeg. Use flour sufficient to make a soft dough. Mix expeditiously, roll thin, and bake in a quick oven.

Cocoanut Cookies.

One cup grated cocoanut, 1½ cups sugar, ¾ cup butter, ½ cup milk, 2 eggs, 1 large teaspoonful baking powder, ½ teaspoonful extract of vanilla, and flour enough to roll out.

Ginger Snaps.

Two cups molasses, 1 cup lard or butter, 2 teaspoonfuls soda dissolved in 2 tablespoonfuls hot water, and 1 teaspoonful each of ginger and cinnamon. Mix as soft as can be rolled, and bake in a hot oven.

Two cups molasses, 2 cups brown sugar, 1 cup butter and lard together, 4 cups flour, 2 tablespoonfuls ginger, 1

CAKES. 83

tablespoonful each of cloves, cinnamon and allspice, ½ a nutmeg, and 1 teaspoonful soda dissolved in hot water. Do not crowd them in the pans, and bake in a moderate oven.

Ginger Cookies.

One cup brown sugar, 1 cup molasses, 1 cup lard, 1 cup hot water, 1 teaspoonful soda, 1 teaspoonful ginger, and ¼ teaspoonful powdered alum put in last. Mix as soft as can be rolled, and bake in a quick oven.

Vanilla Cookies.

One cup sugar, ⅔ cup butter, 2 eggs, 3 teaspoonfuls baking powder and 1 of vanilla, and 1 tablespoonful milk ; add flour enough to roll out.

Soft Molasses Cake.

One cup butter, 1 pint molasses, 1 pint flour, ½ pint milk, 2 eggs, 1 tablespoonful ginger, 2 teaspoonfuls soda; flour enough to make not quite as stiff as cup cake. Bake in moderate oven.

Sponge Cake.

Pour 1 cup boiling water over 2 cups sugar; separate the yolks and whites of 4 eggs and beat both well, the whites to a stiff froth; add the yolks to the sugar and hot water, beating quickly, then 2 cups flour, in which 1½ teaspoonfuls baking powder have been sifted; add a small pinch of salt and 1 teaspoonful lemon extract. Lastly, add the whites of the eggs, mixing as lightly as possible ; bake in a quick oven.

Angels' Food.

This is a very delicate cake, every condition of which must be strictly observed, or it will prove a failure. Take 1¼ tumblers pulverized sugar, or the very fine granulated, 1 tumbler flour, whites of 10 eggs, 1 teaspoonful cream tartar, and 1 teaspoonful extract of lemon or vanilla. Beat the whites to a stiff froth; then sift sugar, flour and cream of tartar together, four times, so as to make it extremely light. Stir in quickly the whites, and with as little beating as possible. Put into an unbuttered tin—one with a pipe in the centre is preferable—and bake 40 minutes in a slow oven. Turn upside down to cool, but put something under the edges to prevent its lying on a flat surface, or it will be apt to become heavy.

White Sponge Cake.

One and a half tumblerfuls granulated sugar, 1 tumblerful flour, the whites of 2 eggs beaten to a froth, 1 teaspoonful each of cream tartar and vanilla extract. Sift the flour three or four times before measuring it. Bake quickly.

Delicate Cake.

One cup butter, 2 cups sugar, ½ cup sweet milk, 4 cups flour, or enough to make a moderately stiff batter, 2 teaspoonfuls baking powder, and whites of 7 eggs beaten to a froth. Flavor with lemon, rose or almond. Bake in shallow pans.

Gold Cake.

One and one-half cups sugar, ½ cup butter, 1 cup sweet milk, 2 teaspoonfuls baking powder, 3 cups flour, yolks of 6 eggs. Flavor with nutmeg.

Silver Cake.

One and one-half cups sugar, ½ cup butter, 1 cup sweet milk, 2 teaspoonfuls baking powder, 3 cups flour, whites of 6 eggs beaten to a froth. Flavor with bitter almond.

Macaroons.

One-half pound sugar, ½ pound shelled almonds, and the whites of 2 eggs. Put the almonds into hot water until the

CAKES. 85

skins slip off easily; then dry, and beat or pound them fine in a mortar, adding a little rose water to moisten them; then add the sugar. Beat the whites to a very stiff froth, and add them to the above. With a little flour on the hands, mould them into little cakes. Bake in a moderately hot oven.

Soft Gingerbread.

One cup molasses, ½ cup butter, 1 cup boiling water poured on the butter and molasses, 2 cups flour, 1 teaspoonful soda, ½ teaspoonful ginger, a small pinch of cloves and 1 egg.

Corn Starch Cake.

One cup butter, 2 cups sugar, 2 cups flour, 1 cup corn starch, 1 cup milk, whites of 7 eggs, 2 teaspoonfuls baking powder. Flavor with rose or almond.

Citron Cake.

One cup butter, 3 cups sugar, 4 cups flour, 5 eggs, the whites and yolks beaten separately, ½ pound of citron, finely cut, 1 teaspoonful lemon extract, 2 teaspoonfuls baking powder.

Pound Cake.

One pound sugar, 1 pound flour, 1 pound butter, whites of 8 eggs. Beat the whites and yolks separately. Flavor to taste. Bake in a moderate oven. These are nice baked in small pans.

Cup Cake.

Three eggs, 1½ cups sugar, ½ cup melted butter, 1 cup water, 3 cups flour, 3 teaspoonfuls baking powder. Bake in layers if desired.

Chocolate Cake.

Two cups sugar, 1 cup butter, 1 cup sweet milk, 5 eggs, 3 cups flour, 2 teaspoonfuls baking powder. Rub butter and sugar to a cream, and beat the whites and yolks separately. Divide the dough, and put the whites in one part and the yolks in the other. Flavor the white with rose or lemon, and the yellow with nutmeg. Bake in jelly pans, two of each kind. Filling : 3 tablespoonfuls grated chocolate, ½ teacup sugar, as much boiling water, 1 teaspoonful corn starch, butter size of a hickory nut. Cook until it thickens; when cold, flavor with vanilla. Put alternate layers of yellow and white.

Rich Fruit Cake.

Two pounds sugar, 2½ pounds flour, 1½ pounds butter, ¾ pound citron, 2 pounds each of raisins and currants, 1 oz. mace, 6 eggs, ½ cup milk, 1 nutmeg, 1 teaspoonful cloves and 1 of cinnamon, 2 teaspoonfuls baking powder.

Black Cake.

One pound each of flour, sugar and butter, 3 pounds each of currants and raisins, ½ pound citron, 10 eggs, 2 teaspoonfuls each of nutmeg and cinnamon, 1 teaspoonful cloves, 1 teaspoonful baking powder. Brown the flour, and also use part brown sugar.

Bread Fruit Cake.

Take out 2 cupfuls of dough after it has raised the second time, and add 3 cupfuls of white sugar, creamed with 1 of butter, 1 teaspoonful of soda dissolved in a little hot water, 2 tablespoonfuls of milk, 3 eggs. After all are well beaten, add a teaspoonful each of cinnamon and cloves, and ½ pound of currants.

Marble Cake.

One and one-half cups sugar, ½ cup each of milk and butter, 2½ cups flour, 2 teaspoonfuls baking powder, whites of 4 eggs beaten to a stiff froth. Flavor with lemon. This is for the white part. The dark part: 1½ cups brown sugar, ½ cup

CAKES. 87

butter, ¼ cup milk, yolks of 4 eggs well beaten, 2¼ cups flour, 2 teaspoonfuls baking powder, 1 teaspoonful each of cinnamon and allspice, ¼ teaspoonful black pepper and half a nutmeg. Bake one hour if in one loaf. The white and dark parts may be baked in alternate layers, or by putting in a tablespoonful of each color, in turn, till all is in.

Cocoanut Kisses or Cones.

One grated cocoanut, whites of 2 eggs, 1 cup powde sugar. Beat the whites stiff, add sugar, then cocoanut. M: into cones with the hands, or by pressing them into little pa forms. Bake in a moderate oven.

Hickory-Nut Cake.

Two cups sugar, 1 cup butter, 1 cup water, 4 eggs, 3 cups flour, 3 teaspoonfuls baking powder, 2 cups hickory-nut meats, chopped fine. Flavor to taste. Bake in a loaf.

Lady Fingers.

Four ounces of sugar, yolks of 4 eggs well beaten, 3 ounces flour, a little salt. Beat the whites to a froth, and stir them in with the mixture, a little at a time, till all is in. Butter a shallow pan, and squirt them through a little piece of paper rolled up, or a confectioner's syringe. Dust with sugar, and bake rather slowly.

Spice Cake.

One cup sugar, 1 cup molasses, ⅔ cup butter, 1 cup sour milk, 3 cups flour, 3 eggs, 1 teaspoonful each of soda, nutmeg and cloves, ½ teaspoonful cinnamon.

Orange Cake.

Two cups sugar, ¼ cup water, yolks of 5 eggs, whites of 3, grated rind and juice of 2 oranges, 2 cups flour, 3 teaspoonfuls baking powder, a little salt. Bake in four cakes, and put between them and over the top frosting made of 2 cups sugar, 2 eggs, the rind and juice of 1 orange.

Crullers.

Two cups sugar, 2 cups new milk, butter the size of an egg, 3 teaspoonfuls baking powder, 3 eggs. Flavor with nutmeg and cinnamon. Mix enough flour with them to roll out without sticking.

Cream Doughnuts,

One and a half cups sugar, 2 cups cream, 2 eggs, flour enough to roll out; 2 teaspoonfuls baking powder if the milk is sweet, or, if sour, 1 each of soda and cream tartar. Roll quite thin; cut out in rings.

White Cake.

Two cups sugar, $\frac{3}{4}$ cup butter, 1 cup sweet milk, $1\frac{1}{2}$ cups each of corn starch and flour, 2 teaspoonfuls baking powder. Flavor with lemon. Whites of 6 eggs, beaten to a froth, and added last. Bake in moderate oven.

Jumbles.

One cup butter, $1\frac{1}{4}$ cups sugar, 2 eggs, 1 teaspoonful baking powder, dissolved in a tablespoonful of milk. Use flour enough to roll out thin. Sprinkle sugar on the moulding-board, and a little over the top in rolling out. Bake quickly.

Queen Cake.

One pound of flour, $\frac{1}{2}$ pound of butter, $\frac{1}{2}$ pound of sugar, 3 eggs, 1 teacupful of cream, $\frac{1}{2}$ pound of currants, 1 teaspoonful of soda, essence of lemon or almonds to taste. Work the butter and sugar to a cream, add the well-beaten eggs, and the cream with the dissolved soda, and lastly the flour. Beat all well together, and bake in small pans from $\frac{1}{4}$ to $\frac{1}{2}$ hour.

JAMS AND JELLIES.

In preparing these sweetmeats it is always the best economy to get the freshest fruits possible, and to use the best grades of sugar. The kettles in which they are made should be porcelain-lined, granite ware, or brass or copper, though the last two must be kept polished in order to insure safety in their use. Wooden spoons are better for stirring all acid fruits than iron or other metallic ones.

Strawberry Jam.

Mash the berries with a wooden spoon, or squeeze them lightly with the hand ; place in the preserving kettle and cook 15 minutes. For each measured quart of berries add 1¼ pounds white sugar ; stir well, and boil slowly 25 to 30 minutes.

The above directions for making jam will apply to all the small fruits, as currants, raspberries, blackberries, gooseberries, etc.

Gooseberry Jelly.

Boil the berries in a very little water until they are soft, squeeze them through a jelly-bag ; put the juice into a kettle, and add a cup of sugar to 1 of juice. Boil 15 or 20 minutes, and then pour into glasses.

Red Currant Jelly.

Pick the fruit from the stems, put it in a porcelain kettle over the fire and let it simmer until the juice is well drawn from the currants ; then strain through a jelly-bag ; do not squeeze it too much, or the pulp will be pressed through with the juice and make the jelly muddy. To each pint of juice allow ¾ pound of best white sugar ; put the juice into the kettle, and, when it boils, add the sugar; keep stirring until it is done, removing the scum as it rises. After 20 or 30 minutes put a little into a dish, and, if firm, it is done. Put in jelly glasses, and cover with oiled paper.

Crab Apple Jelly.

Cut the apples in halves, and put in a kettle with as little water as will keep them from scorching. Cover tightly with a lid, and cook quickly. Strain through a jelly-bag, add a cupful of white sugar to each cupful of juice. Set it over the fire and boil until it jellies. It will often jelly in 10 minutes, but it sometimes requires a full half-hour. Try the jelly every 2 or 3 minutes, as the longer it boils the darker it is.

Orange Jelly.

Boil ½ pound of white sugar with ½ pint of water until there is no scum left (which must be carefully removed as fast as it rises); peel the oranges without breaking the thin skin of the inner divisions; put these into the syrup and let them cook 5 minutes; then take them out and use the syrup for the jelly. When the oranges are well drained and the syrup is nearly cold, pour a little of the latter into the bottom of the mould; then lay in a few pieces of orange; over these pour a little jelly, and when this is set, another layer of orange, proceeding thus until the mould is full. Put it on ice or in a cool place, until wanted.

Apple Jelly.

Wash a peck of apples; cut them up with 3 lemons; place in a preserving kettle and cover with water. Boil until they can be mashed; then put in a jelly-bag to drain. The jelly will be clearer if they are not squeezed. Measure the juice, and take as much sugar as juice. Boil the juice hard 25 minutes, and skim; then add the sugar, and boil briskly 10 minutes,

PRESERVING FRUIT.

Tomato Preserves.

To have good preserves the tomatoes should be about a third ripe. Remove the skin with a very sharp knife, for the thinner the peeling the more whole the tomatoes will remain. Pour into a preserving kettle enough water to cover the bottom an inch deep. Measure the tomatoes and put them into the kettle; add as much sugar as tomatoes, and let them cook slowly for several hours. The syrup must be thick and the preserves a rich brown.

Rhubarb, or Pie Plant.

Peel and cut it in small pieces, cover it with boiling water, let it stand five minutes, then pour off all the water and put the rhubarb on the fire in a kettle with a little water, and a cupful of sugar to each bowlful of the fruit. After it has boiled slowly for 10 minutes, put into glass jars, and seal while hot. Glass is better than tin for rhubarb, which is very acid and may attack the tin.

Canning Currants.

Place the fruit in the kettle with very little water, and as soon as they begin to boil, add ½ pound sugar for each quart of berries. Boil 6 minutes; remove from the fire and put into cans.

Dried Rhubarb.

Prepare the same as for pies, by peeling the stalks and cutting into pieces an inch long. Spread it on plates, not pans, and place in a warm oven. It should dry quickly, and then be put away in paper bags.

PICKLES.

Pickles should not be kept in glazed or tin ware; stone jars or wooden casks are preferable. The vinegar should be either of wine or cider, as made vinegars are unreliable and unhealthful. It should not be too strong, or it will eat the pickles.

Cucumber Pickles.

Select the medium, small-sized cucumbers. Soak in brine, not too salt, for 2 or 3 days. Dry them, and put in wide-necked bottles or jars; then to 1 gallon cider vinegar add 2 cups sugar, a small handful whole cloves, a half cupful white mustard seed, a couple roots of horse radish cut fine, 3 or 4 green peppers, with seeds removed, and a piece of alum the size of a butternut. Heat these ingredients, and pour over the pickles. Repeat, heating the vinegar three consecutive days, and each time pour it hot over the pickles. Seal them in glass bottles, and they will require no further attention.

Pickled Cauliflower.

Break the heads into small pieces, and boil 10 or 15 minutes in salt and water; remove from the water and drain carefully. When cold, place in a jar, and pour over it hot vinegar, in which has been scalded a liberal supply of whole cloves, pepper, allspice and white mustard. Tie the spices in a bag, and, on removing the vinegar from the fire stir into each quart of it two teaspoonfuls French mustard.

Chopped Tomato Pickle.

Chop fine a peck of green tomatoes, a head of cabbage, a few green peppers, and 3 heads of celery. Mix salt through them, a teaspoonful of salt to each cupful of pickle; let them stand over night, then turn upside down on a board to drain. Add enough vinegar to cover the chopped pickles, a teaspoonful of mustard, one of pepper and a few slices of horse radish. Boil five minutes, then pour hot over the chopped pickle.

Pickled Onions.

Peel small onions, and let them lie one day in salt and water. Scald ten minutes in milk and water. Let them drain well, and then put them in wide-necked bottles. Pour hot spiced vinegar over them. Cover closely.

Martynia Pickles.

Gather the pods before they form any woody fibre, scald them in salt and water till they are tender; drain well, and pour over them spiced vinegar. Cover, and let them stand a few days before using.

Piccalilli.

One gallon chopped cabbage, 2 quarts each chopped green tomatoes and onions; ½ pound brown sugar, two ounces white mustard seed, 2 tablespoonfuls salt, ½ ounce each of pepper, celery seed and allspice, 1 teaspoonful cloves, 2 quarts vinegar. Boil till the cabbage, etc., are tender. Then bottle and seal.

Chili Sauce.

To 1 peck ripe tomatoes, pared and chopped, add ¼ as many peppers, 3 cups sugar, 2 quarts vinegar, 3 tablespoonfuls salt. Boil 2 hours. Bottle and cork or seal tightly. Add 2 or 3 onions if preferred.

Sliced Tomato Pickles.

Slice 1 peck of green tomatoes, and a few small onions, put in a jar, and sprinkle over them a little salt; let them stand over night, then drain. Take a quart of vinegar, some pepper pods chopped fine, 2 tablespoonfuls of mustard, a teaspoonful of ground cinnamon, a teaspoonful of ginger and ½ a teaspoonful of black pepper. Heat the vinegar, add the spices, and when it comes to the boil add the tomatoes. Let them boil 4 minutes, then pour into a stone jar.

Pickled Peppers.

Cut out the stems and seeds with a sharp knife. Fill the peppers with chopped cabbage, grated horse radish, mustard seed, small radish pods and salt. Replace the stem after cutting off the seeds; tie it on firmly. Pack in a jar, and cover with cold vinegar.

Sweet Tomato Pickles.

One peck ripe tomatoes; 4 lbs. of brown sugar, 1 qt. of cider vinegar, 1 oz. each of stick cinnamon and cloves; tie the spices in a muslin bag. Make a syrup of the vinegar, sugar and spices, then put in the tomatoes and boil until tender, keeping them as whole as possible; boil the syrup 3 or 4 hours longer, or until quite thick; place in jars; when cold, seal up.

Spiced Crab Apples and other Fruits.

For 7 lbs. of crab apples use 3½ lbs. sugar, 1 qt. best vinegar, 2 ozs. of stick cinnamon, 1 oz. of whole cloves, and 2 or 3 pieces of root ginger. Boil the syrup fifteen minutes before putting in the apples, cook until tender; then remove to glass or stone jars, boil down the syrup one-half, and pour over the apples.

N. B. Most other common fruits, as apples, pears, peaches, cherries, currants, gooseberries, etc., may be prepared by the same method as given for crab apples, varying the spices, sugar and vinegar as needed.

EGGS.

Scrambled Eggs.

Separate the yolks and whites, beat the former well, and pour into a hot buttered spider; season with a little salt and pepper. When the yolks are partly cooked, pour in the unbeaten whites. Stir a little, so as to mix the white with the yellow yolks somewhat. A little chopped parsley mixed with the yolks is preferred by many.

Poached Eggs.

Have ready, in a spider, boiling water, slightly salted. Drop into this, from a saucer, each egg as broken, being careful not to crowd them in the vessel. With a spoon, dip the water up over them until the yolks are coated; then remove them, carefully laying each on a slice of buttered toast.

Bachelor's Omelet.

Make a thin cream of ½ teacupful of milk, 1 teaspoonful of flour, and 3 well-beaten eggs. Salt and pepper to taste. Place 2 ounces of butter in a pan, and, when very hot, pour in the batter. Let it remain a few minutes over a clear fire, then sprinkle upon the omelet some fine-chopped herbs and a few bits of onion; double it upon itself, and remove to a hot platter.

Shirred Eggs.

As each egg is broken, slip it into a small buttered egg-cup, or oval side-dish, strew salt and pepper over the top, and set in a hot oven for three or four minutes. Serve in the dish in which they are baked.

VEGETABLES.

Mashed Potatoes.

Peel carefully, boil in salted water, until done. Pour off the water, and let them drain perfectly dry. Season with butter, salt, and hot milk or cream, then take a large fork or spoon and stir vigorously until they are white and creamy. In this state, they are still further improved by rubbing them through a colander, and serving without further mixing.

Boiled Potatoes.

The water should always be salted, and boiling, when they are put in, and not be allowed to stop boiling until they are done, when it should be poured off immediately, and the kettle put on the back part of the stove, with the cover off, and the potatoes allowed to dry for a few moments before serving.

Warmed-Over Mashed Potatoes.

To 2 cupfuls of the cold potato add a cupful of milk, a tablespoonful butter, 2 tablespoonfuls flour, and 2 eggs beaten to a froth. Mix the whole with the cold potato until it is thoroughly light, then put it into a pudding-dish, and bake to a golden brown. The quality depends upon very thoroughly beating the eggs before adding them, so that the potato will remain light and porous after baking, almost like sponge cake.

Egg Plant.

Cut it in slices about ⅜ of an inch thick. Soak in weak salt water over night. Before cooking, dry on a towel, dip in beaten egg, and roll in bread or cracker crumbs. Have ready a spider or pan, with hot drippings and butter, or all

VEGETABLES.

butter, if one prefers, and fry slowly, so as to be sure and have the plant thoroughly cooked, otherwise it is very tasteless. When a rich brown, serve, and send to the table hot.

Saratoga Chips.

Peel and slice as many potatoes as are needed for a meal. Put them into cold water ½ hour before they are to be cooked. Dry a handful at a time on a napkin, and drop them into hot lard. Stir while cooking, to keep them separate. When yellow, take up on white paper, till drained; sprinkle salt over them, and send to the table hot.

Stewed Corn.

Cut carefully from the cob, and add just enough water to cover it. Cook from 20 to 30 minutes, then season with butter, pepper, salt, and add milk or cream, hot.

Corn Fritters.

To a quart of corn add 2 eggs well beaten, 2 tablespoonfuls flour, 1 teaspoonful salt, ½ teaspoonful pepper. Have ready a kettle of hot lard, drop the corn from the spoon into the fat. Fry a light brown.

Succotash.

Take double the amount of corn that you do beans. Cook the beans ½ hour before adding the corn, in just enough water to keep them from adhering to the kettle. Season with a plentiful supply of butter, pepper and salt, and add a little milk.

Hubbard and Marrow Squashes.

Hubbard squashes are generally preferred baked, as their rinds are so hard they can not be peeled easily. They require an hour or more to bake well. Boston marrow and similar varieties should be pared and cut up in small pieces, and steamed or boiled. When tender, mash, adding butter and salt. A small quantity of thick sweet cream added is a great improvement.

Green Corn Griddle Cakes.

One pint of milk, 2 cups grated green corn, a little salt, 2 eggs, a teaspoonful baking powder, flour sufficient to make a batter to fry on the griddle.

Summer Squash.

Cut them in quarters, tie the pieces in a thin muslin bag, and boil in slightly salted water until tender. Then remove from the kettle, and with a ladle press out all the water. Take out of the bag, put into a spider, mash fine, and add butter, pepper and salt to taste. Let it simmer, and serve while hot.

Salsify.

Scrape off the outer skin of the salsify, and cut it into thin pieces. Boil an hour or more, as it should be very soft in order to be good. When done, put in a little salt codfish, picked very fine, having previously let the water boil nearly away, add plenty of milk to make a gravy, and season with salt, pepper and butter. Thicken the gravy a little, and, when serving, add small bits of toast.

Salsify Patties.

The roots are cooked soft, mashed, and seasoned with a little butter, pepper and salt, and then made into small cakes, rolled in flour, and fried in hot fat or butter.

Stewed Celery.

Break apart and wash very carefully three heads of good celery; cut the celery into thin pieces, and boil in salted water. When tender, drain and place neatly on a vegetable dish,

VEGETABLES.

sprinkling over it some black pepper. Pour off part of the water; wet into a smooth paste 1 teaspoonful each of corn starch and flour, 2 tablespoonfuls of butter and the same of rich cream; stir this into the water, over the fire, till it thickens, and then pour over the celery.

Cauliflower.

Boil it very tender in water, slightly salted; then drain well, and have ready either a drawn butter sauce to pour over it, or a white sauce, made of milk, thickened with a little flour and seasoned with butter, pepper and salt.

Cream Cabbage.

Cut very fine, put it into a sauce-pan, and cover with water; when tender, drain off the water, add butter, salt and pepper, and a cupful of cream. Let it scald; then serve.

Peas.

Boil in water enough to cover them well. When done, which will be in about half an hour, add milk or cream, butter, pepper and salt. When the milk is thoroughly scalded, they are ready for the table. Serve while hot.

Tomatoes a la Creme.

Pare and stew a quart of ripe tomatoes until smooth. Season with salt, pepper and a tablespoonful of butter. When done, add one cup sweet cream and a little flour. Let it scald, but not boil; remove at once. Pour over slices of toast.

Scalloped Tomatoes.

Stew and season a quart of tomatoes as for the table. Have ready as much bread crumbs and a little chopped onion. Place in a pudding dish alternate layers of the tomato and bread crumbs, seasoning with salt, pepper, plenty of butter, and a very little of the onion. Let the last layer be bread crumbs. Bake in a good oven 20 or 30 minutes.

Baked Tomatoes.

Select a dozen smooth, solid tomatoes; cut a slice from the blossom end, and scoop out a portion of the pulp; season bread crumbs with butter, pepper and salt, and enough cream to moisten the crumbs. Fill the tomatoes with them, place in a pan, add a little water to keep them from burning, and bake.

Asparagus.

Break off the stiff portions, and place the green, soft parts into boiling water, slightly salted. Cook until tender; drain off the water, make a drawn butter gravy and pour over it. Some prefer a white sauce, and have toasted bread laid on the platter before pouring on the sauce.

Beets.

They are simply boiled until perfectly tender, cut in thin slices, and served with butter and salt, or with vinegar poured over them, and used as pickles. When preparing beets for cooking they should never be cut at all, since otherwise the sweet juice boils out into the water and makes them tasteless.

Cold Slaw.

A cabbage knife cuts it very evenly, but without this it can be sliced very fine; add a little sugar, salt and pepper, and pour cold vinegar over all.

Lima Beans.

Shell, wash, and put into boiling water with a little salt; when boiled tender, drain and season them, and either dress with cream or a large lump of butter, and let them simmer for a few moments.

MISCELLANEOUS.

To Remove Oil or Grease Spots from Carpets.

Lay a piece of blotting paper over the spot, and set a flat iron on top, the iron just hot enough not to scorch. Change the paper as often as it becomes greasy. After the most of the oil has been extracted, apply whiting; leave it on for a day or two, then brush off, and the spot will have disappeared.

To Remove Mildew from Cloth.

Put a teaspoonful of chloride of lime into a quart of water, strain it twice, then dip the mildewed places in this weak solution; lay in the sun; if the mildew has not disappeared when dry, repeat the operation.

Cleaning Soiled Gloves.

The best way to clean any color of kid gloves is to pour a little benzine into a basin and wash the gloves in it, rubbing and squeezing them until clean. If much soiled they must be washed through clean benzine, and rinsed in a fresh supply. Hang up in the air to dry.

A Remedy for Mosquito Bites.

Put 10 drops of refined carbolic acid into an ounce of rose water, shake well, and apply as needed. This has been in use several years, and proves cooling to the most tender skin.

To Color Red.

Take 1 ounce of cochineal, 1 ounce of muriate of tin, and a little cream of tartar for each pound of goods, dissolved in enough water to cover them. Boil the goods in the dye for 10 minutes. Hang up to drain and dry.

Paste for Scrap Books, etc.

Dissolve a lump of alum as large as a hickory nut in a quart of boiling water. Mix ½ a pint of flour to a smooth, thick batter, stir in the alum water, and boil 5 to 10 minutes, until the paste looks smooth and transparent, then remove from the fire, and stir in a small teaspoonful each of oil of cloves and of sassafras.

Cement for Glass.

A good, clear cement for glass is hard to find. One is made by dissolving an ounce of isinglass in 2 wine-glasses of spirits of wine. Care must be taken not to let it boil over, as it is highly inflammable.

Washing Colored Calicoes.

Dissolve say 10 cents' worth of sugar of lead in 6 to 8 quarts of pure water (rain water is best), and, after the garments are washed and rinsed, let them be dipped in and wrung out. It not only sets the color, but keeps it.

Durable Whitewash.

Fresh, well-slaked lime, stirred into equal parts of water and buttermilk, to the usual consistency, will make a whitewash that will not rub off. Keep it hot while applying it.

Washing Flannels.

The proper way to wash woolen garments or socks, is to rub them gently through *warm* suds made of white hard soap, with a teaspoonful of powdered borax to each two gallons. Rinse in clear, warm water, and dry quickly.

To Raise the Pile of Velvet.

Cover a hot iron with a wet cloth, and hold the velvet over it. Brush it quickly while damp, to raise the pile.

Iron Rust and Ink Stains.

Rub lemon juice on the stain, then cover it with salt, and lay the articles in the sun. If necessary, repeat the process two or three times. Spots from most kinds of ink are similarly taken out. Vinegar will sometimes do it.

To Get Rid of Moths.

Sprinkle furniture and cushions thoroughly with benzine. It will not spot or injure the most delicate fabric, but is sure death to moths. The work *must* be done in a place where there is neither a fire nor a lighted lamp, for the benzine is very explosive.

To Clean Marble.

Take 2 parts of common soda, 1 part of pumice stone, and 1 part of finely powdered chalk; sift it through a fine sieve, and mix it with water; then rub it well all over the marble, and the stains will be removed; wash with salt and water.

Setting Colors.

To set the color in blue lawn, dissolve three cents' worth of saltpetre in a pailful of water, and dip the lawn in it several times before washing.

To Drive Away Ants.

A little quicklime placed in the infested places will drive away any kind of ants.

Insect powder, which can be bought at any drug store, sprinkled around the infested place, will keep away all kinds of insects.

To Keep Dolls from Breaking.

It has been proved by experience with several dolls that filling the entire head with wet plaster of Paris, and allowing it to set firmly, will render the head almost indestructible.

Cleaning a Hair Brush.

Dissolve a little soda in warm water, and pour in a small amount of ammonia (liquid hartshorn), which you can get at any store. Hold the brushes with the bristles downward, and avoid wetting the back as far as possible; shake until the grease is removed. Then rinse in cold water, and put in the air to dry.

To Clean Silverware.

Do not use soap in cleaning silver. When it wants polish, rub it with whiting on chamois skin.

To Remove Stains from Linen.

Wet the part stained, and lay on it some salt of wormwood; then rub without diluting it with more water.

Homemade Vinegar.

Put in an open cask 4 gallons of warm rainwater, 1 gallon of common molasses, and 2 quarts of yeast; cover the top with thin muslin, and leave it in the sun, covering it up at night and when it rains. In 3 or 4 weeks it will be good vinegar.

To Remove Tar from Cloth.

Rub it well with turpentine, and every trace of tar will be removed.

Washing Fluid.

One can of the best concentrated lye, 5 cents' worth of salts of tartar, 10 cents' worth of ammonia dissolved in 1 gallon of water. Put in a jug, and cork tightly. To use it, wash the clothes through one suds first; then put nearly a quarter of a teacupful of the mixture to a boiler full of clothes. Boil thoroughly 20 minutes; then remove, and rinse the clothes in two waters.

www.ingramcontent.com/pod-product-compliance
Lightning Source LLC
Chambersburg PA
CBHW031411160426
43196CB00007B/979